GREAT
AMERICAN
ASTRONAUTS

GREAT AMERICANS ASTRONAUTS

BY CHRIS CROCKER

FRANKLIN WATTS
NEW YORK/LONDON/TORONTO
SYDNEY/1988

Back cover photographs courtesy of NASA

Photographs courtesy of:
UPI/Bettmann Newsphotos: pp. 17, 20, 23, 35, 101.
All other photographs courtesy of NASA.

Library of Congress Cataloging-in-Publication Data

Crocker, Chris, 1959-
Great American astronauts.

Bibliography: p.
Includes index.
Summary: Presents the lives and careers of ten
well-known astronauts and highlights some of the famous
"firsts" in the history of the United States space program.
1. Astronauts—United States—Biography—Juvenile
literature. [1. Astronauts. 2. Astronautics—History]
I. Title.
TL789.85.A1C76   1988   629.45'0092'2 [B]   87-29560
ISBN 0-531-10500-8

Thanks to helpful friends Jim Lyons,
Jean Rosenbluth, Annene Kaye,
Simon Gillham, June Honey, and,
above all, Jane Friedman.

Special thanks to the National
Aeronautics and Space Administration
for their assistance in the preparation
of *Great American Astronauts*.

CONTENTS

GREAT
AMERICAN
ASTRONAUTS

1

PROJECT MERCURY

In the first half of the twentieth century, the new science of rocketry was largely undeveloped. Yet, by the end of the Second World War, the most advanced rocket research had been done by German scientists. Their V-2 rocket was the first missile to travel faster than sound, raining death on London with unheard-of speed and power. After the defeat of Nazi Germany, both the victorious Americans and Russians enlisted captured German scientists for their respective rocket programs.

In the early days of the Cold War between the United States and the Soviet Union, rocket research was less concerned with scientific discovery than with the construction and deployment of missiles with sufficient power to send nuclear warheads to targets on the other side of the world. The use of rockets to send people into space was not the primary concern of rocket scientists. The value of space travel and satellite technology was hotly debated in the United States during the 1950s, but on October 4, 1957, the Soviet Union gave the American space program the biggest boost in popularity it ever dreamed possible.

It was on that day that the USSR launched the world's first artificial satellite into earth orbit. Named *Sputnik 1*, the 22-inch (56-cm) -wide metal sphere woke America up to the fact that the Soviet Union was a scientific, as well as military, force to be reckoned with. A Russian satellite flying over our cities made a lot of people nervous. Soviet Premier Nikita

Khrushchev heightened American anxieties by telling the *New York Times* three days after the launch that his nation had "every kind of rocket required for modern war."

AMERICA LOOKS SPACEWARD

Up to that point, one of America's several space agencies had been the National Advisory Council on Aeronautics. President Dwight Eisenhower proposed the formation of a civilian space agency, the National Aeronautics and Space Administration (NASA), on April 2, 1958. On July 29 of that year, President Eisenhower signed the National Aeronautics and Space Act, which set the stage for NASA's existence. NASA officially came into being on October 1, 1958.

Situated 35 miles east of Orlando, Florida, is Cape Canaveral, home of what is now the Kennedy Space Center. On July 24, 1950, the first rocket was launched from Cape Canaveral.

The announcement of Project Mercury to a Sputnik-scared American people came on December 17, 1958—exactly fifty-five years to the date from the Wright brothers' historic flight at Kitty Hawk, North Carolina. The goals of the Mercury program would be to send a man into space and to study the effects of space flight on the human body. Building on the knowledge provided by Project Mercury, far more complex missions would follow in the years ahead.

THE MERCURY ASTRONAUTS

When NASA initiated the astronaut program, it drew up a set of basic requirements, which were met by 508 men. Every candidate had to be a military jet test pilot who was still on active duty with a minimum of 1,500 hours of flight time. Even their personal statistics had to conform to NASA guidelines. All astronauts had to be 5 feet 11 inches (180 cm) or shorter and not older than forty. Over months of rigorous testing and evaluation, the number of candidates for the Mercury program was brought down from 508 to seven. (In the selection of subsequent astronaut groups in the years to come, restrictions on height and age were loosened somewhat.)

The Mercury astronauts. Front row (left to right): Walter Schirra, Donald Slayton, John Glenn, Scott Carpenter. Back row (left to right): Alan Shepard, Virgil Grissom, Gordon Cooper.

The seven pioneering astronauts, who were officially presented to the American public on April 9, 1959, were Alan Shepard, Virgil Grissom, John Glenn, Scott Carpenter, Walter Schirra, Gordon Cooper, and Donald Slayton.

THE FIGHT FOR CONTROL

When NASA scientists referred to the space vehicle they created as a "capsule," the Mercury astronauts strongly objected. They called it a "spacecraft," something that takes a pilot to fly it.

Mercury astronaut Donald "Deke" Slayton recalled in the television documentary *Spaceflight,*

> *When we came on board there was one little porthole down by the hatch. The hatch screwed on—there was no way to get it off. Ninety to one hundred screws in the darned thing that had to be put on for launch and taken off to get you out of there post-launch. So the first three things we did: We got a window put up in front of the pilot so he could see and have some visibility to effectively control the machine. Then we had a control system in it that allowed us to control it. And then the third thing was we got a hatch that would blow off, so you could get out of the darned thing.*
>
> *It was designed at that time to operate totally unmanned and did operate unmanned, of course, the first couple of flights—with chimps in 'em as a matter of fact—and we got used to there being a chimps-were-the-test-pilots-and-we-were-the-guys-following-behind kind of thing, you know. Which rankled people a little bit.*

Christopher Columbus Kraft, who was the flight director of Project Mercury, knew it would be a mistake to make the spacecraft operational only from the ground. As he stated in *The Space Program Quiz & Fact Book,* "Man is the deciding element. . . . As long as man is able to alter the decisions of the machine, we can perform under any known conditions."

THE MERCURY ROCKETS

The most crucial and suspenseful moment of any rocket launch is the countdown. The tension of astronauts, flight controllers, and spectators alike heightens as the countdown reaches zero: ". . . three

Freedom 7, *the first Mercury spacecraft, is launched into space.*

. . . two . . . one . . . ignition!" The countdown is a tradition that only exists in the space program—and it has its origins in science fiction. When pioneering German scientists of the 1920s and 1930s launched a rocket, they counted backward to zero because they'd seen it done in the old science fiction film *Woman in the Moon*. The film's director, Fritz Lang, had decided to count backward for his "rocket launch" because he thought it was more dramatic that way.

The first rocket designated to launch the manned Mercury capsule was the Redstone. One of the earliest American rockets, the Redstone had much in common with the German V-2. It had enough thrust to send a Mercury capsule out of the atmosphere at a speed of 5,200 miles (8,400 km) per hour, but not enough to put the capsule into orbit.

THE MERCURY SPACECRAFT

The Mercury capsules were the first American spacecraft in space, but they were bell-shaped and likened sometimes to a flying tin can, nothing like the needle-sharp rockets of science fiction movies in the 1950s, whose shape many scientists thought was the right one for a spacecraft. One space engineer, H. Julian Allen, realized that a spacecraft needed a blunt end to slow the capsule down when it hit the atmosphere and to reduce the intense heat of reentry. A capsule resembling a science fiction rocket would have burned up as soon as it tried to get back home.

Manufactured by the McDonnell Aircraft Company, the Mercury capsules were only 9 feet (2.7 m) long and a little over 6 feet (1.8 m) across at their widest point, and weighed 3,200 pounds (1,450 kg).

The nose of the Mercury capsule contained the parachutes for splashdown, and the capsule's base was a heat shield that would protect the astronauts from the friction-generated heat of reentry. The angle of reentry into the earth's atmosphere is of crucial importance. If the spacecraft approaches the atmosphere at too steep an angle, it will burn up in the outer atmosphere. If, on the other hand, the craft approaches the earth at an angle that isn't steep enough, it will actually "skip" off the atmosphere, much as a stone skips on the surface of a lake. In this case, the craft would shoot off into space again, making another attempt to reenter impossible or, at best, extremely difficult.

THE OTHER MERCURY FLIGHTS

The historic space flights of Alan Shepard and John Glenn are told in later chapters, but the other Mercury missions were also important. They would lay the groundwork for other "firsts" to come.

After Alan Shepard's flight, Virgil "Gus" Grissom made the second suborbital flight in the Mercury capsule *Liberty Bell 7*. Like Shepard's, Grissom's flight was another well-executed fifteen-minute space shot. The only moment of danger for Gus Grissom came after the capsule had splashed down. While the *Liberty Bell 7* bobbed in the Atlantic surf waiting for the rescue helicopter, the explosive escape hatch blew off accidentally. Water rushed into the capsule and, in his bulky spacesuit, Grissom barely escaped drowning. His capsule sank to the bottom of the Atlantic.

Scott Carpenter's *Aurora 7* flight was the next orbital mission after John Glenn's. Carpenter performed a good number of experiments in orbit—he viewed it as a scientifically oriented flight. While he was occu-

Mercury astronaut Scott Carpenter

THE MERCURY MISSIONS

No.	Astronaut	Craft Name	Launched
MR-3	Alan Shepard	*Freedom 7*	May 5, 1961
MR-4	Gus Grissom	*Liberty Bell 7*	July 21, 1961
MA-6	John Glenn	*Friendship 7*	February 20, 1962
MA-7	Scott Carpenter	*Aurora 7*	May 24, 1962
MA-8	Wally Schirra	*Sigma 7*	October 3, 1962
MA-9	Gordon Cooper	*Faith 7*	May 15, 1963

pied with his observations, his fuel supply was dwindling. By the time Carpenter reentered the atmosphere, he was completely out of propellant. What really frightened NASA controllers was the fact that the *Aurora 7* went out of communication for four hours. Many at NASA thought that Carpenter had reentered the atmosphere at the wrong angle and burned up. Walter Cronkite, covering the event on TV, said, "I'm afraid we may have lost an astronaut." Soon, NASA discovered that Carpenter's capsule had splashed down safely, but it was 250 miles (400 km) off target.

After the Carpenter mission, NASA would not let Mercury astronauts do as much controlled maneuvering experimentation in orbit. Wally Schirra's *Sigma 7* flight was to help the astronauts concentrate on economical use of propellant. Schirra's nine-hour, six-orbit flight was deemed "letter perfect" by flight directors; *Sigma 7* had proven how maneuverable the Mercury craft was.

The final flight of the Mercury program was Gordon Cooper's *Faith 7* mission. Orbiting around the earth twenty-two and a half times, this flight set the endurance record for the program—over thirty-four hours in orbit. Still, the *Faith 7* craft had experienced a number of failures. By the end of the flight, nearly all of Cooper's automatic controls had failed. He was flying the capsule manually until splashdown. His splashdown in the Pacific was perfect. The flying abilities of Gordon Cooper kept disaster from striking the final Mercury mission. This achieved once and for all one great goal of the Mercury astronauts: to prove that an astronaut was a *pilot*, fully in charge of a spacecraft. The Mercury astronauts weren't just "spam in the can."

ALAN B. SHEPARD, JR.
First American in Space

When Alan Shepard rode a fiery Redstone rocket into suborbital space flight on May 5, 1961, he raised the hopes of the American people and he raised the ante in the U.S./Soviet space race. After the flight of *Freedom 7*, Alan Shepard's career would encompass disappointments as well as triumphs—he would meet with presidents and walk on the moon.

NEW HAMPSHIRE AND THE PACIFIC WAR ZONE

Alan Bartlett Shepard, Jr., was born on November 18, 1923, in East Derry, New Hampshire. After attending primary and secondary schools in East Derry, Shepard attended Admiral Farragut Academy, where he first distinguished himself as a leader. Alan next attended the United States Naval Academy at Annapolis. In 1944, Shepard graduated from Annapolis with a bachelor of science degree.

At that time the United States was engaged in World War II, and Shepard immediately went into active duty, fighting in the Pacific on the Navy destroyer U.S.S. *Cogswell*. After the war, he took civilian flying lessons before entering naval flight training at Corpus Christi, Texas, and Pensacola, Florida. In 1947, he "received his wings"; he was designated a naval aviator. He served in the Navy's fighter squadron 42, flying Corsair aircraft from the deck of the aircraft carrier U.S.S. *Franklin D. Roosevelt*, which patrolled the Mediterranean.

The brown-haired, blue-eyed Shepard married Louise Brewer of Kennett Square, Pennsylvania. Alan and Louise Shepard would raise two daughters, Laura and Julie. A seasoned naval aviator and new father, Alan Shepard returned to college to join the elite class of aviators—a test pilot.

After his graduation from United States Navy Test Pilot School in Patuxent River, Maryland, Shepard worked on a large number of Navy projects, such as high-altitude tests to investigate air masses over North America and changes in light at different altitudes. He worked on in-flight refueling techniques, the risky business of filling a plane's gas tank while it's racing through the skies at high speeds. He later moved to California, where he became operations officer for a squadron of night-fighting Banshee jets. This Banshee squadron made two tours of the western Pacific on the aircraft carrier U.S.S. *Oriskany.*

Returning to Patuxent River for a second tour of duty, Shepard test-piloted some of the hottest aircraft of the 1950s. In 1957, he graduated from the Naval War College in Newport, Rhode Island, and went on to serve as aircraft readiness officer on the staff of the commander-in-chief of the Atlantic Fleet.

THE MERCURY YEARS

As a Mercury astronaut, Alan Shepard knew that he was a "front-runner" to be the first man in space. As he told *Spaceflight,* "I don't think it would be a surprise to you to find out there was a tremendous amount of competition. . . . It was interesting in that all of us *did* work together—in the engineering aspect we each had separate assignments and we would have meetings and could bring in things that we had discovered or learned or re-designed or changed—in the early days. So, there was the camaraderie associated with that, but on the other hand, each one of us knew that only one guy was gonna have the first flight, though. The competition was there—underlying everything."

It was announced on February 21, 1961, that the first flight would be made by either Shepard, Grissom, or Glenn. Flight directors wanted to keep the name a secret as long as possible, but three days before the launch, word had leaked out. Alan Shepard would be the first American to ride a rocket into space.

Alan Shepard, the first man in space,
greets well-wishers on his return to earth.

THE *FREEDOM 7* FLIGHT

Alan Shepard named his Mercury capsule *Freedom 7*, and in so doing created the tradition of putting the numeral 7 after each of the Mercury capsule names. According to Shepard, he chose 7 because it stood for capsule number 7 which rode on top of booster number 7 for the first of seven Mercury flights. Seven turned out to be the wrong number, since there would ultimately be only two suborbital flights and six flights altogether.

On the morning of his historic liftoff, Shepard started the prelaunch tradition of a steak-and-eggs breakfast. Most astronauts followed suit and ordered the same thing throughout the early years of the space program. (This tradition has had its ill effects as well. Astronaut Neil Armstrong was quoted as saying "I'm sick of steak" after two aborted launches, which were preceded by two big steak suppers.[1])

Alan Shepard sat confidently in his capsule on the morning of the launch, even though he had made the proper "financial arrangements" if he didn't survive the flight. After repeated countdown delays, his mood turned restless. At one point, after the countdown had been held, he pointedly asked mission control, "Why don't you fix your little problem . . . and light this candle?"[2]

The Redstone rocket lit up perfectly at precisely 9:34 A.M., sending Shepard on a "ballistic trajectory," which is a lot like a manned bullet. The Redstone shot Shepard 116 miles (187 km) above the earth and into the heavens. As the Redstone went from subsonic to supersonic speeds, the capsule vibrated somewhat, but smoothed out after a few moments. When the fuel in the Redstone was exhausted, the booster separated from the Mercury capsule. If the booster rocket didn't blast free of the capsule, it would fatally complicate reentry. At the moment when the capsule broke loose from the rocket stage, Shepard's pulse rate rose to 132— the highest it would be for the entire mission. (NASA doctors wired astronauts with multiple sensors to monitor their physical reactions to space flight.)

Shepard didn't have much chance to marvel at outer space during his Mercury flight. "Most of the time, something's happening," he told *Spaceflight*. "You're either launching or you're reentering or you're maneuvering in space and you don't have a lot of time to think about—on that flight I had about thirty seconds in which to look around and gaze upon the earth from that altitude. See what it looked like and make some kind of profound statement."

After the booster was jettisoned, Shepard experienced weightlessness for the first time while *Freedom 7* was traveling at a speed of 4,500 miles (7,250 km) per hour. At this point, he switched the craft over to manual

*The Redstone rocket leaves a vapor trail as it
boosts the Mercury capsule into the atmosphere.*

control. He found that the Mercury craft could be steered by its hydrogen peroxide jets. As Alan Shepard told *Life* magazine, "I took over control of the roll motion of the capsule and was flying *Freedom 7* on my own. This was a big moment for me and for everybody who had worked so hard on Project Mercury. Major Gagarin may have had a fine long ride but, as far as we can tell, he was a passenger all the way."

When the Mercury capsule had reached its highest point, Shepard fired the retro-rockets as the craft began to descend. He didn't need to fire them to make his reentry—he fired them as a test for later orbital flights where the retro-rockets would be crucial for reentry. As each retro fired, the angle of the craft was altered a bit, but Shepard proudly used the controls to keep his capsule stabilized.

As Shepard's mission was drawing to a close, there was only one thing that malfunctioned: a signal light. While the light indicated that Shepard's retro-pack was still attached to the capsule, he himself saw the pack drop off into the ocean below.

"In that long plunge back to earth I was pushed back into the couch with a force about ten times the pull of gravity," Shepard told *Life*. As he reentered the earth's atmosphere, the heat reached 1500°F (815°C) outside the capsule and 102°F (39°C) inside the cabin. By the time *Freedom 7* dropped to 30,000 feet (9,000 m), it was going 300 miles (483 km) per hour and was right on target for splashdown in the Atlantic. At 21,000 feet (6,400 m), the small *drogue chute* opened, followed by the main chute at 10,000 feet (3,000 m). At the end of his fifteen-minute flight, a helicopter from the aircraft carrier U.S.S. *Lake Champlain* picked up Alan Shepard and *Freedom 7* 302 miles (486 km) downrange from his launch site. Aboard the carrier, Shepard received a congratulatory telephone call from President John Kennedy. America's first manned space shot had been a success.

AFTER MERCURY

After his celebrated flight, Alan Shepard was given a ticker-tape parade in New York, saluted at the White House, and presented with an honorary master of arts degree from Dartmouth College. He described his reactions to fame to *Naval Aviator News*: "In the beginning there was a lot of glamour and excitement. It was new to the public. But there really wasn't that much to it. John Glenn went through a lot more than I did."

Alan Shepard wanted very much to fly the last Mercury mission in the capsule *Freedom 7 II*. NASA thought the flight was unnecessary, but NASA director James Webb told Shepard that if President Kennedy OK'd the flight, he could close out the Mercury program. Kennedy said the decision was NASA's, and so the capsule never flew. *Freedom 7 II* now belongs to the National Air and Space Museum.

In 1963, Alan Shepard became Chief of the Astronaut Office. He was in charge of anything that involved the astronauts, from evaluating spacecraft to deciding which experiments would be performed in space.

Shepard had been selected for one of the first Gemini flights when he started experiencing a dizziness that came and went unpredictably. NASA doctors diagnosed the cause as an inner ear infection, and he was barred not only from space missions but from flying airplanes without another pilot present.

He told *Naval Aviator News*, "The difficulty was termed Meniere's syndrome, a form of dizziness. The problem is not considered very significant for an earthbound person, but it sure can finish you as a pilot. I convinced myself that it would eventually work itself out. But it didn't." In fact, the hearing in Shepard's left ear was actually deteriorating.

Fellow astronaut Tom Stafford told Shepard about a doctor in Los Angeles who performed an operation to correct Meniere's disease. In 1968, Shepard went to California from his home in Houston and registered at the hospital under the name Victor Poulis.[3] Shepard didn't want

*New York City gives Alan Shepard and
his wife a ticker-tape parade.*

word to get out that he was having his ear operated on—he couldn't bear the thought of get-well messages pouring into his hospital room.

Months after the operation, Alan Shepard was finally considered cured of Meniere's disease, with almost all the hearing coming back into his left ear. After a few medical tests, he was returned to astronaut flight status in 1969.

THE TRIP TO THE MOON

Shepard was assigned as commander of the *Apollo 14* mission to the moon. He took long hours to train for the mission. He described his training to *Life*: "The human mind can only comprehend so many details, and when you stuff more things into the memory bank other things are bound to dribble out. . . . You ought to try to cram it as full of the right things as you can right up to the last moment."

There were those who thought Shepard was assigned the flight more because of his authority than for his ability. "Nobody said to me: 'Look, you're too old, you've been away from it too long. Forget it,' " he told *Life*. "Nobody said that directly, but indirectly I've sensed that there are certain people who felt that maybe the old guy shouldn't be given a chance."

The crew of *Apollo 14* was a "rookie" crew. The only space flight time any of them had logged was Shepard's, and he'd only been up for about fifteen minutes! Along with crewmates Stuart Roosa and Edgar Mitchell, Shepard blasted off for the moon on January 31, 1971. After the *Apollo 14* lunar landing vehicle set down on the moon with Shepard and Mitchell, they set up a number of lunar experiments. On the moon, Shepard amused the world by swinging a long-handled soil-collection scoop with a golf club head attached and hitting a golf ball into a crater. The astronauts also used the Mobile Equipment Transporter, a kind of outer space wheelbarrow, to collect 94.6 pounds (42.9 kg) of moon rocks, which they later brought back to earth. All in all, Shepard spent nine hours and seventeen minutes walking on the lunar surface.[4]

Alan Shepard had come back from losing some of his hearing and being grounded from space flight. Now he was coming back from the moon. On February 9 the *Apollo 14* capsule returned safely to earth and was recovered in the Pacific by the carrier U.S.S. *New Orleans*. In July 1971, President Richard Nixon assigned Shepard to be a delegate to the twenty-sixth United Nations General Assembly, where he served until December of that year. He continued to work as Chief of the Astronaut Office until his resignation from both NASA and the Navy on August 1, 1974. Since that time, Alan Shepard has been involved in private business in Houston, Texas.

JOHN H. GLENN, JR.
First American to
Orbit the Earth

John Glenn's Mercury mission to orbit the earth tackled the first great obstacle of space flight and made him a celebrity on a scale greater than that of Alan Shepard. In the course of his flight, Glenn would encounter space phenomena that had never been seen before and would come very close to becoming America's first fatality in the heat of reentry.

THE MAN FROM OHIO

John Herschel Glenn, Jr., was born in Cambridge, Ohio, on July 18, 1921. John grew up in the town of New Concord, where he attended grade school and high school. As a young man, he enrolled at Ohio's Muskingum College, but dropped his studies to fight as a marine in World War II. At about this same time, Glenn married Anna Margaret Castor, whom he had known since his school days in New Concord. In the years that followed, the Glenns had two children, John David and Carolyn Ann.

In the Marines, John Glenn entered the Naval Aviation Cadet Program and graduated the next year. He joined Marine Fighter Squadron 155, where he flew F4U fighters on fifty-nine combat missions in the Marshall Islands.

Still on active duty after the war ended, Glenn flew in Fighter Squadron 218, which patrolled northern China. He returned to the United States in 1948 and became an instructor in advanced flight training at Corpus Christi, Texas. After a course in amphibious warfare in Quantico,

Virginia, John Glenn went to war again, this time in Korea. He flew sixty-three missions in the Marine Fighter Squadron 311, and an additional twenty-seven missions while an exchange pilot with the Air Force.

After the Korean War, Glenn attended Test Pilot School at the Naval Air Center in Patuxent River, Maryland. He was next assigned to the Fighter Design Branch of the Navy Department of Aeronautics. At this time, Glenn set an airspeed record from Los Angeles to New York—three hours and twenty-three minutes. In that same year, 1957, many Americans got their first look at John Glenn. He was a contestant on the TV quiz show *Name That Tune* for two weeks.[1]

THE FLIGHT OF *FRIENDSHIP 7*

Among his fellow Mercury astronauts, John Glenn was certainly liked, but he had a reputation for strict personal and professional discipline that others often viewed as extreme. Glenn was the sole straightbacked marine in an astronaut group made up of more casual Navy and Air Force men. (The other Mercury astronauts had a fondness for fast sports cars and would make fun of Glenn for driving a slightly beat-up car.)

Nonetheless, it was John Glenn who was chosen to be the first American to orbit the earth. The *Friendship 7* flight was originally intended to be the third and final suborbital flight of the Mercury program, but NASA scientists felt that enough was understood about space flight from the previous Shepard and Grissom flights to attempt the first orbital mission. On February 20, 1962, the Atlas booster sent John Glenn into earth orbit on a column of fire.

Glenn's orbit was looked upon as the first answer to a number of medical questions, as so little was known about orbital flights and weightlessness in those days. As John Glenn told *Spaceflight*:

> It sounds very elementary right now, but on my flight . . . one of the basic things I was to come back with were measurements, hopefully, on what happens to man's senses in space flight. And there were some doctors at that time who wrote very seriously about the fact that in weightlessness for a number of hours, your eyes would no longer need to be supported by the structure under your eyes, and the muscle structure there. And would your eyes change shape slowly, as you're in orbit for a while? And would this wreck your vision?
>
> Some of the doctors had predicted that in the weightlessness of space flight, the fluids of your inner ear would be moving in just random motions, instead of being held down by gravity as they are

Left: *John Glenn leaving the Cape Canaveral hangar on his way to the launch pad.* Below: *Glenn squeezes aboard the tiny capsule.*

right here. And they felt that when these random motions occurred, it might make you so nauseous you would not be able to even make an emergency reentry if you found it necessary to do that. I carried along with me little tablets to take if I started feeling a little queasy. And then they had designed a syringe with a spring-loaded needle. If I found I needed this I could take it out and take the safety catch off and hit my leg with it and it would drive the needle through the suit, into my leg and inject the fluid."

None of these strange effects of space ever struck John Glenn, however. He reportedly found weightlessness "pleasant—you could become an addict."

John Glenn would witness even stranger effects in outer space—little glowing particles that sailed past his capsule window. No one had expected to see those bright cinders in space that he referred to as "fireflies." Glenn was so interested in these little firefly particles that he used the manual controls and turned the capsule around 180 degrees to get a better look at them.[2]

This is the description Glenn gave at his debriefing at Grand Turk Island the day after his flight: "I could see nothing but luminous specks about the size of stars outside. I realized, however, they were not stars. . . . The specks were luminous particles that were all around the capsule. There was a large field of spots that were about the color of a very bright firefly, a light yellowish-green color." On a later Mercury flight, Scott Carpenter identified the luminous particles as ice crystals and bits of oxidized paint from the capsule's exterior. Known as "the Glenn effect," these space "fireflies" have been reported by American and Soviet space travelers alike.

After flying across the globe from sunlight into shadow, Glenn said, "That was about the shortest day I've ever run into." And not long before he reentered the atmosphere, Glenn sent an unexpected message to fellow astronaut Gordon Cooper, back on earth. "Hey Gordon, I want you to send a message for me," Glenn radioed. "Send a message to the commandant of the U.S. Marine Corps that reads: 'Have four hours' required flight time. Request flight check be prepared for me. Signed John Glenn, Lieutenant Colonel, U.S. Marine Corps.'" Although this message was strictly for a laugh, John Glenn actually received $245 in flight pay for his orbital mission. (Alan Shepard got only $14.38 for his suborbital flight.)[3]

During his three orbits of the earth, Glenn's craft developed some trouble with the altitude-control thrusters. At this point, he gladly took manual control of the capsule. But the real emergency of his flight occurred when a signal flashed at an island-based tracking station that

Through his capsule window, Glenn watched glowing specks fly past.

the heat shield on Glenn's capsule may have been coming loose. Loss of the heat shield would have proved disastrous when he encountered the fiery heat of reentry into the atmosphere. Without the shield, Glenn would have been burned to a cinder.

The housing for Glenn's braking rockets, or retro-pack, was held on by metal straps stretched across the heat shield. Ordinarily, these rockets would be jettisoned after they were fired. Mission Control hoped that if only Glenn *did not* jettison his retro-pack, the thin metal straps would prevent the heat shield from slipping off. The flight controllers didn't want to alarm Glenn that something was wrong, but when they told him to leave the retro-pack on, he realized that there was trouble with the heat shield.

These are the words exchanged between John Glenn and Mission Control:

MC: "We are recommending you leave the retro-package on through the entire reentry. Do you read?"
JG: "This is *Friendship 7*. What is the reason for this? Do you have any reason? Over."
MC: "Not at this time."

Glenn later told *Spaceflight*: "It didn't take any brilliant deduction to know that they were indicating that they'd had a signal that something was wrong. And I was a little aggravated at the time that they didn't just come right out and tell me what it was."

Glenn was referring here to his initial disappointment with Mission Control, because eventually, just before reentry, they did tell him what the problem was.

When *Friendship 7* reentered the atmosphere, pieces of the burning retro-pack sailed past Glenn's small window.

"Boy, that was a real fireball," is how he described it to ground controllers.

John Glenn recalled those tense moments in *Spaceflight:*

It made a very spectacular reentry from where I was because once I had started reentry and the high heat then started burning these parts of the retro-pack off, they started coming back past the window where I was looking out. . . . I could see these big burning chunks coming back. And at that time I couldn't be absolutely certain whether it was the retro-pack or the heat shield that was tearing off. . . . I can remember, though, thinking that if it's

*the heat shield tearing up, I'm gonna feel the hot heat on my back
very soon. . . . It didn't do any good to panic at that point.*

Then Glenn radioed, "This is *Friendship 7.* I think the pack just let go."
Fortunately, the heat shield held in place, and Glenn splashed down very
near the recovery ship. Glenn hurt his hand blowing open the Mercury
escape hatch, but was otherwise in good shape after his flight. He
reported, "My condition is excellent."

Recovered in the Atlantic by the U.S.S. *Noa,* Glenn came home to a
wave of celebrity that was even more intense than Alan Shepard's had
been the year before. The nation was proud of John Glenn; at last an
American had orbited the earth and returned home safely. A number of
babies born around the time of his flight were named in his honor. Rumor
has it that one Utah newborn was actually named Orbit in honor of the
Friendship 7 flight.[4]

THE SENATOR FROM OHIO

When John Glenn addressed a joint session of Congress on February 26,
1962, he charmed the nation with his insistence on sharing the spotlight
with his wife, children, parents, in-laws, and fellow NASA personnel.
Looking to the future, John Glenn told the president, congressmen, and
dignitaries, "We look forward to Project Gemini—a two-man orbital
vehicle with greatly increased capability for experiments. There will be
additional rendezvous experiments in space, technical and scientific
observations—then, Apollo orbital, circumlunar and finally, lunar landing
flights." While pointing ahead to the future of space travel, John Glenn
may have been indirectly pointing at his own future in the U.S. Congress.

In 1964, John Glenn became the first astronaut to retire from the
Manned Spacecraft Center (what is now the Johnson Space Center). On
January 1, 1965, he retired from the Marine Corps. He became a highly
paid executive for Royal Crown Cola.

John Glenn's political aspirations started after his resignation from the
Marines. He wanted to gain the nomination of the Ohio Democratic Party
to run for Congress, but an accidental fall in the bathroom at home left him
sidelined until future elections.

After repeatedly seeking a way into Congress, Glenn was nominated
by the Democrats to run for the Senate in 1974. John Glenn joked about
the spaceman image that voters might have of him to the *Saturday Eve-
ning Post:* "I think there might have been a question in some people's

Glenn returned to earth a hero.
Here, Glenn (center, back seat) rides
in a parade with President John Kennedy
and Air Force General Leighton Davis.

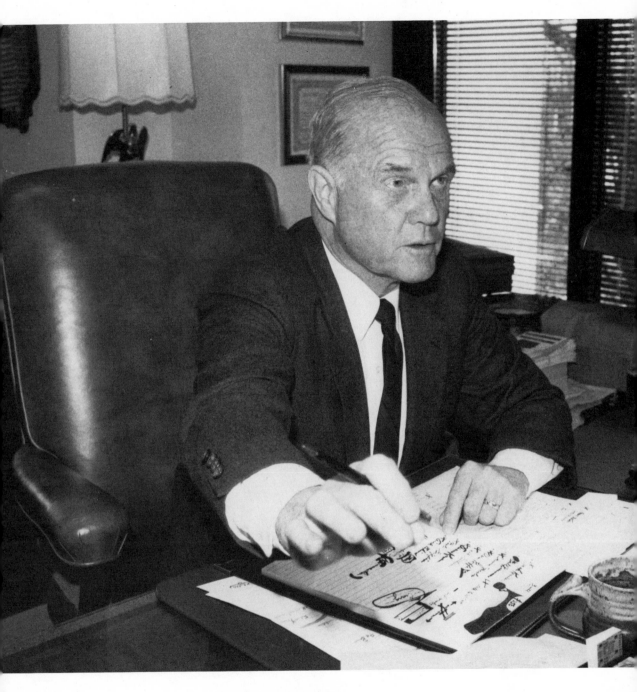

Senator John Glenn in his office
on Capitol Hill

minds whether, because of my background, I might come here with one big eye in the middle of my forehead, or pointed ears or something."

Glenn continued to say that he thought it was "high time the Senate included someone with a background in science or engineering or technology, since more than half the decisions we make have to do with the physical sciences in some way."

On Election Day, 1974, John Glenn defeated the Republican candidate, Cleveland Mayor Ralph J. Perk, to become the first astronaut in the United States Senate. (To date, the only other astronaut to serve in the Senate has been Harrison Schmitt, who served from 1977 to 1983.)

PROJECT GEMINI

Gemini, the two-man space project, was named after the twins of classical mythology who were called the Gemini. An interim program to prepare for Project Apollo, Project Gemini would provide extremely valuable information for subsequent space flights. The space agency stated the most important goals of this new project as:

1. To subject a two-man crew to the isolation of long periods in earth orbit
2. To have two space vehicles perform the first rendezvous (in which two crafts almost touch in space) and docking (in which they then link up in space)
3. To test the effects of astronauts going outside of the capsule for "spacewalks," or extravehicular activity (EVA)
4. To perfect methods of reentry into the earth's atmosphere.[1]

THE GEMINI SPACECRAFT

The Gemini program was started to develop and fly a spacecraft that was equipped with *attitude-control* thrusters, small rockets that change the direction of a capsule in space. With each firing of the thrusters, the Gemini capsule could actually be steered in space, instead of following a preset trajectory, like a bullet.

Although larger in size, the basic shape of the Gemini capsule wasn't much different from that of Mercury. The rear of the capsule, the adapter module, contained the sixteen thrusters that made the Gemini a truly maneuverable craft. The crew compartment, known as the reentry module, was 11 feet (3.4 m) high and 7½ feet (2.3 m) across at the capsule's widest point.

John Young recalled the Gemini capsule in *Spaceflight*, saying,

The Gemini was very small and compact. For a while there we called it a "Gusmobile" because Gus [Grissom] was really the only guy that could get in it and close the hatch without it hitting him on the top of the head—it was that crowded. It was like sitting sideways in a phone booth—it was really tight. It was a pilot's spaceship—every control in there was right at your fingertips. The displays were just optimum for the job we had to do, which was ascent, entry and rendezvous.

On every space mission, there is one principal contact at Mission Control whom the astronauts speak to most of the time. This person is designated as the capsule communicator, generally known as CapCom. The CapCom is always another astronaut—someone who can best understand space flight and the vehicles involved. Another important reason that an astronaut must work as CapCom: the astronauts know their jobs and each other very well. Another astronaut might be able to spot emotional nuances in a fellow astronaut's voice that a flight director wouldn't notice. There is an astronaut-CapCom for every manned space flight.

THE OTHER GEMINI MISSIONS

Gemini 3, piloted by Gus Grissom and new astronaut John Young, demonstrated the remarkable maneuverability of Gemini, the first true manned spacecraft. Although the first Gemini flight lasted less than five hours, it proved that the new spacecraft could effectively change its orbit, a vital step toward the rendezvous and docking experiments to come.

Only one Gemini spacecraft had a special name (like the Mercury capsules before them and Apollo modules that were to follow). Gus Grissom called *Gemini 3* the *Molly Brown*, named after the hit Broadway musical *The Unsinkable Molly Brown*. This was a clear joke on Grissom's Mercury capsule, which sank after splashdown. NASA officials were reportedly unamused at the nickname. But at launch, CapCom Gordon Cooper said, "You're on your way, *Molly Brown*!" and it quickly caught on with the

THE GEMINI MISSIONS

No.	Astronauts	Launched
3	Virgil "Gus" Grissom, John Young	March 23, 1965
4	James McDivitt, Edward White	June 3, 1965
5	Gordon Cooper, Charles Conrad	August 21, 1965
6-A	Walter Schirra, Thomas Stafford	December 15, 1965
7	Frank Borman, James Lovell	December 4, 1965
8	Neil Armstrong, David Scott	March 16, 1966
9-A	Thomas Stafford, Eugene Cernan	June 3, 1966
10	John Young, Michael Collins	July 18, 1966
11	Charles Conrad, Richard Gordon	September 12, 1966
12	James Lovell, Edwin "Buzz" Aldrin	November 11, 1966

press and public alike. And incidentally, *Gemini 3* lived up to its new name when it splashed down in the Atlantic.

After Ed White's historic *Gemini 4* spacewalk, Gordon Cooper and Charles Conrad took *Gemini 5* into orbit for additional testing. They tried out a newly designed fuel cell, which malfunctioned. They also tried a docking maneuver—without the target rocket. This imaginary target would be a dry run for a real rendezvous in the future. Since Agena rockets were designated to be the unmanned "target vehicles" in the Gemini program, the crew of *Gemini 5* chased the "Phantom Agena" throughout earth orbit. Astronauts Cooper and Conrad also confirmed what many other astronauts had said before: that things like oceangoing ships and Cape Canaveral itself were plainly visible from orbit—a height that many had thought was too great to distinguish anything on the ground. Their observation contributed significantly to the common use of satellites to spy all over the world from orbit.[2]

The launch of *Gemini 6* has been delayed a number of times, once nearly ending the lives of Tom Stafford and Wally Schirra. It was eventually launched as *Gemini 6-A*. While the troubled *Gemini 6* sat on the ground, *Gemini 7* took off for orbit carrying astronauts Frank Borman and

Jim Lovell. Nine days later, *Gemini 6-A* was launched and proceeded to perform the first manned rendezvous with *Gemini 7*. During this mission, Borman and Lovell would set a space endurance record of 330 hours— over thirteen days in a very cramped Gemini capsule.

Gemini 8, flown by rookie astronauts Neil Armstrong and David Scott, was the first in-flight near-disaster of the American space program. After successfully docking with an Agena rocket, the Gemini spun out of control. Armstrong and Scott managed to control it by piloting skills alone. The mission was called off early, and the *Gemini 8* capsule splashed down after less than eleven hours in orbit.

After the troubled docking of *Gemini 8*, astronauts Tom Stafford and Gene Cernan would dock *Gemini 9-A* with an orbiting rocket. The rocket's *payload* shrouds were supposed to unfold like gigantic flower petals for docking with the Gemini. Unfortunately, they jammed, making docking impossible. The half-opened payload shrouds were likened to an "angry alligator" by frustrated astronaut Tom Stafford. During the same mission, Cernan walked in space, but had a great deal of physical difficulty once he was outside the capsule. This made NASA doctors aware that there were quite a few problems associated with spacewalking.

Second-time astronaut John Young and rookie Michael Collins took *Gemini 10* into two different orbits and successfully docked with two separate Agena target vehicles. On each, Collins performed an extravehicular activity. He was the first astronaut to step outside the spacecraft *twice* during one flight, and he experienced many of the same EVA problems that Gene Cernan had experienced on the previous flight.

Charles Conrad and Richard Gordon, as the crew of *Gemini 11*, executed another perfect orbital docking with an Agena target vehicle. Conrad and Gordon also distinguished themselves as the first to create artificial gravity. Since there is no gravity in space, *centrifugal force* can be used to simulate something "pulling" in one direction. The Gemini craft and the Agena were attached by 100 feet (30.5 m) of Dacron tether line. As the two orbiting vehicles spun slowly around each other, Conrad noticed that a TV camera had "fallen down" in the direction of the centrifugal force.

The crew of Gemini 12, *Jim Lovell (left, in cap) and Buzz Aldrin, are welcomed aboard the U.S.S. Wasp after splashdown.*

The last mission of Project Gemini was *Gemini 12*, with astronauts Jim Lovell and Edwin "Buzz" Aldrin. On this flight, Buzz Aldrin helped to work out the problems of EVAs, and what was learned would benefit astronauts for years to come. When *Gemini 12* splashed down on November 15, 1966, a great deal had been learned about changing a spacecraft's orbit, rendezvous and docking with another orbiting vehicle, and even walking in space. All of these Gemini program advances would directly benefit the next phase of the space program: Project Apollo and the first voyage to the moon.

EDWARD H. WHITE, II
First American to
Walk in Space

When he set foot outside his *Gemini 4* spacecraft in June 1965, Ed White had the greatest view of any American in history. He could see not only the earth passing magnificently below, but also the limitless heavens above. Before Ed White's bold and treacherous steps into the vacuum of space, astronauts had viewed the universe through a tiny window. White's walk through space would extend the view and expand the horizons of the American space effort.

THE TEST PILOT FROM TEXAS

Edward Higgins White, II, was born in San Antonio, Texas, the son of an Air Force major general who had not only flown aircraft but had operated Army balloons as well. After his years of schooling in San Antonio, Ed attended the United States Military Academy at West Point, where he set a school record in hurdles, as well as ran every day and played soccer. He graduated with a bachelor of science degree in 1952. After West Point, he received flight training in Florida and Texas. For three and a half years, Ed White flew F-86 and F-100 aircraft while stationed in Germany.

In 1959, Ed White received a master's degree in aeronautical engineering from the University of Michigan. The same year, he enrolled in the Air Force Test Pilot School at Edwards Air Force Base. Graduating as an experimental test pilot, White was assigned to fly at Wright-Patterson Air

Force Base with its Aeronautical System Division. While at Wright-Patterson, Ed White made flight tests for research and weapons systems development, wrote technical engineering reports, and submitted recommendations for improving aircraft construction and design.

Ed White was sometimes the pilot of the specially equipped plane that NASA uses to simulate zero gravity for future astronauts. The plane flies on what's called a *parabolic curve*, in which an aircraft drops at a rate that makes the occupants of the plane essentially weightless. This plane has also been known as the "Vomit Comet" for the effect that sudden weightlessness has had on some trainees.

THE *GEMINI 4* MISSION

Ed White was one of the second group of astronauts to be accepted by NASA. Chosen in September 1962, the nine Group 2 astronauts also included John Young and Neil Armstrong. White's first flight was to be Gemini 4, commanded by fellow Group 2 astronaut Jim McDivitt.

The name that Ed White had originally wanted for Gemini 4 was *American Eagle*, *Phoenix*, or *Little Eva*. The last name was a clever play on EVA and the name of a popular rock singer of the time, Little Eva, who had a big hit with the song "The Loco-Motion." Ultimately, the craft would have no official name.

On June 3, 1965, *Gemini 4* raced into orbit under the power of a Titan II launch vehicle, which was much more powerful than the Atlas rocket that was used before it. Ed carried with him a small United Nations flag which his father had kept while serving with U.N. peace-keeping forces during the Korean War. (After White returned to earth, he gave the well-traveled flag to U Thant, who was then secretary-general of the United Nations.) Although the flight of *Gemini 4* would set an American space record of four days and sixty-two earth orbits, it was during the third orbit that Ed White began his extravehicular activity.

In a pressurized spacesuit with a shaded sun visor, Ed White eased himself out of his side of the close-quarters Gemini capsule, firmly attached by 24-foot (7.3-m) -long gold-plated umbilical tether line. In one hand he held a jet-operated maneuvering gun. Since White was floating

Ed White floating in space outside the Gemini 4 spacecraft, his maneuvering gun and his umbilical line in his hands

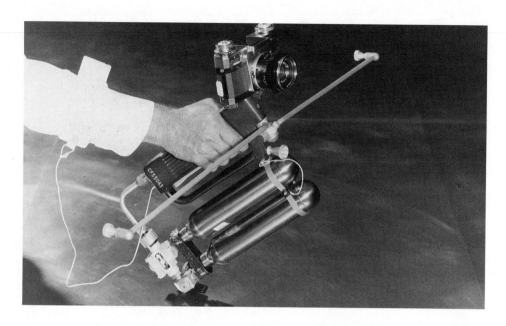

*A hand-held maneuvering unit like the one
used by Ed White during his spacewalk*

freely in space, the little jet of air from the gun would propel him in the opposite direction. By manipulating the two triggers on the gun, Ed White could fly in any direction. He radioed back to Mission Control:

> *My maneuvering unit is good. The only problem that I have is that I haven't got enough fuel. I've exhausted the fuel. I was able to maneuver myself down to the bottom of the spacecraft. I'm looking down now and it looks as if we're coming up on the coast of California. I'm going in slow rotation to the right. There is absolutely no disorientation.*

"One thing about it when Ed gets out there and starts whipping around—it sure makes the craft tough to control," Jim McDivitt remarked from within the capsule.

The television networks covered the White spacewalk live. The only problem was that there was no capacity for live television transmission from Gemini capsules. Still, on some TV screens you could see a "simulated" spacewalker in some earthbound studio trying to enact what White was doing at that moment in space.

At one point during his spacewalk, White had drifted over to the front of the Gemini craft and Jim McDivitt took out his Hasselblad camera to take White's picture. The following is what ground controllers heard the men saying:

JM: "Hey, Ed. Smile."
EW: "I'm looking right down your gun barrel, eh?"
JM: "Let me take a closeup. . . . You smeared up my windshield, you dirty dog! You see how it's all smeared up there?"
EW: "I did? Well, hand me out a piece of Kleenex and I'll clean it."

Literally a man caught between the earth and the heavens, Ed White described what he saw to the world below: "The sun in space is not blinding but it's quite nice. . . . I can sit out here and see the whole California coast. . . ."

White was on a limited air supply, and flight directors thought the twenty-three-minute EVA had gone on just about long enough. This is White and McDivitt's conversation:

JM: "They want you to get back in now."
EW: (laughing) "I'm not coming in. . . . This is fun!"
JM: "Come on."
EW: "Hate to come back to you, but I'm coming."
JM: "Gosh, you still got three and a half more days to go, buddy. . . . C'mon. Let's get back in here before it gets dark."
EW: "I'm hesitating."
JM: "Come on now."
EW: "It's the saddest moment of my life."

It wasn't easy for Ed White to end what has to be among the most exhilarating experiences imaginable, but it was no easier climbing back into the cockpit of the Gemini capsule. He told *Life*:

> *You just don't jump back in a spacecraft as you would into an automobile. We had to go through in reverse the same things we had done to get outside. I had to dismount the camera . . . stow the cable that had been attached to the camera, take off the umbilical guard and get it out of the way, stuff the umbilical cord back into the cabin out of the way of the hatch, hand the maneuvering gun to Jim, and then climb back in backward in my bulky suit and settle down in my seat again.*

Although spacewalking is great fun, it is nevertheless a dangerous activity. If only one crucial piece of apparatus should fail, the astronaut would surely die. Should the Gemini spacesuit become punctured in some way—either by a sharp piece of equipment or by a *micrometeoroid*—the oxygen would rush out of the spacesuit and the astronaut would instantly perish. If the umbilical line were severed in some way and the spacewalker drifted away from the craft, there would be nothing to stop him from floating helplessly through space, waiting for his oxygen supply to run out.

The most pressing danger of the Gemini EVAs, however, was the chance that an astronaut would lose consciousness while spacewalking. If that happened in the Gemini spacecraft, the other astronaut would not be able to pull the incapacitated spacewalker back into the capsule. There was simply no physical way that one astronaut could shove another bulkily suited astronaut back into the Gemini and close the hatch behind him. If all avenues of rescue had been exhausted, the astronaut in the capsule was authorized to cut loose the paralyzed astronaut outside, close the hatch, and head for home. Fortunately, this scenario has never occurred in the history of space flight.

AFTER GEMINI

Ed White's EVA had created such a sensation that there was a certain amount of talk within NASA about Ed White being named the first man to walk on the moon. In March 1966, White, Gus Grissom, and Roger Chaffee were chosen to fly the first manned mission of the Apollo series, *Apollo 1*. When asked how he felt about flying in the first test of the Apollo craft, Ed White said, "I think you have to understand the feeling that a pilot has, that a test pilot has, that I look forward a great deal to the first flight. There's a great deal of pride involved, in making a first flight."

On January 27, 1967, the three *Apollo 1* astronauts died in a launchpad fire that destroyed the Apollo capsule. Ed White was buried at his alma mater, the United States Military Academy at West Point.

Above, left: *for his spacewalk, Ed White wore an emergency oxygen pack and a gold-plated helmet to protect him from the sun.* Below, left: *the crew of* Apollo 1 *(left to right): Ed White, Virgil Grissom, Roger Chaffee*

WALTER M. SCHIRRA
First Astronaut in
Three Space Programs

Wally Schirra, who participated in the Mercury, Gemini, and Apollo programs, is truly an astronaut's astronaut. His superb flying skills were lauded in Mercury, his cool head and steady nerves were appreciated in Gemini, and his humor was known to the world during his Apollo mission. The career of no other astronaut grew along with the American space program as did that of Wally Schirra.

A TRADITION OF FLIGHT

Wally Schirra was born in Hackensack, New Jersey, on March 12, 1923. Flying was in Wally's blood—his father had piloted fighter aircraft in World War I, and his mother had been a "wing-walker." In the old days of propeller-driven biplanes, airplane stunt shows toured the country. One frequent exploit was that of the wing-walker, who would walk out between the two wings of a biplane and very often perform even trickier stunts from there. Wing-walking was the extravehicular activity of the Age of Flight.

Known as "Rah-Rah" Schirra by his classmates, Wally attended the United States Naval Academy at Annapolis, graduating in 1945. From there he enrolled for the two-year naval flight training at Pensacola, Florida. In the following years, Wally Schirra did the treacherous task of flying jet aircraft from the swaying decks of aircraft carriers. In the Korean War,

Wally Schirra flew multiple combat missions. (During his Mercury flight, Schirra looked down to see lightning darting in and out of rainclouds over Australia. It sent a chill up his spine because it reminded him of the antiaircraft fire directed at him by North Korean forces.) After Korea, Wally Schirra became a test pilot, which would lead him eventually into Project Mercury.

THE FLIGHT OF *SIGMA 7*

Wally Schirra named his Mercury capsule *Sigma 7*. The mathematical symbol sigma is used by engineers to designate the solution to a particular problem, and Schirra hoped that *Sigma 7* would provide answers to NASA's questions about space flight.

When Wally Schirra entered his capsule, he saw that launchpad co-workers had left a set of car keys in the cockpit. In hand-tooled, leather-embossed letters, the keycase read *Sigma 7*.

On October 3, 1962, an Atlas rocket sent Wally Schirra into an orbital trajectory. "The Atlas, the stainless steel sausage I was sitting on top of, could go 'bah-room!' or stray off course," Wally later told *Life*, "I knew there were literally thousands of things that could go wrong. . . . But my instincts as a test pilot told me that *Sigma 7* would not fail—not unless somebody, including me, goofed."

Atlas 8 rocket lifts off, bearing the Sigma 7 *capsule and Astronaut Wally Schirra*

Wally's principal mission aboard *Sigma 7* was to see how well a Mercury capsule could fly in orbit using the minimum amount of propellant. Like all the Mercury astronauts, Wally Schirra was determined to *fly* his spacecraft, not be controlled from the ground. As Schirra told *Life*, "The ground stations or the automatic sequences in the capsule had always kept fairly tight control of the situation. Now they were cut and the people on the ground were trusting me with the works."

Schirra, delighted at how easily the Mercury capsule handled, later said, "I could have parked it on a dime if I had to." He even proved that the craft's engines could be shut down entirely in orbit and it would still stay within its charted path—another fuel-saving idea.

The only problem during the *Sigma 7* mission was that Wally's suit overheated because of a faulty valve, but he managed to fix it before splashdown. He had been so successful at conserving his spacecraft's propellant that he had 25 percent left in his manual tank and 60 percent in his automatic tank at the end of his mission. The safest procedure is to dispose of the caustic fuel early, so Schirra dumped it while the parachute-suspended capsule drifted toward the Pacific.

After having orbited the earth six times in over nine hours, *Sigma 7* fell back to earth in the Pacific; it was the first time a manned capsule had not splashed down in the Atlantic.

RENDEZVOUS WITH GEMINI

The launching of Schirra's second space mission was a trouble-plagued one. Flown by Schirra and Tom Stafford, *Gemini 6* was scheduled to dock with an Agena target rocket on October 25, 1965. Before Schirra and Stafford lifted off, flight directors found out that the Agena had exploded before it reached orbit. The launch was postponed. Then NASA came up with a plan that would put *Gemini 6* and *Gemini 7* in orbit simultaneously, enabling them to perform the first space rendezvous of two manned vehicles. With *Gemini 7* crewed by Frank Borman and Jim Lovell, the dual launches would take place in December of that year.

When the countdown reached zero for *Gemini 6-A*, the Titan rocket failed to ignite and could have exploded at any moment. Knowing this, Wally Schirra had to decide if he would use his escape mechanism, effectively canceling the launch, or sit tight with Tom Stafford, hoping that the rocket wouldn't envelope them in flames. Although he had a strong impression that the engines were "shutting down" safely, Wally Schirra couldn't be sure if this decision would be his last. He and Stafford stayed where they were. "We're just sitting up here breathing," a nervous Wally Schirra told ground controllers. Schirra was right—the rocket was fine.

His steely nerves had saved the mission and earned him the nickname "Mr. Cool."

Three days later, the *Gemini 6-A* craft was launched and, after three orbits of the earth, caught up with *Gemini 7*. For five hours and eighteen minutes, the two Gemini capsules sailed through space at thousands of miles per hour within twelve inches (30 cm) of each other. After a brief but flawless mission, Schirra and Stafford splashed down in the Pacific and were picked up by the aircraft carrier U.S.S. *Wasp* on December 16, 1965.

THE FIRST APOLLO MISSION

Since the *Apollo 1* disaster, the Apollo program had been stalled for the better part of two years. When astronauts Wally Schirra, Donn Eisele, and Walt Cunningham were borne aloft by a Saturn 1B launch vehicle on the morning of October 11, 1968, the prayers of NASA and the nation went up with them. As the radically redesigned *Apollo 7* craft ascended toward orbit, Wally Schirra told Mission Control, "She's riding like a dream . . . . we're having a ball!"

The *Apollo 7* mission spent much of its time testing out the Apollo's navigational, propulsion, control, and electrical systems. Schirra used the command and service modules to rendezvous with the second Saturn 1B rocket stage that had been cast off after its fuel was spent. This was an important exercise, since rendezvous and docking would be the basis of Apollo operations in space.

Even the spacesuits worn by the *Apollo 7* astronauts had been redesigned from the Gemini suits. Each Apollo suit weighed 57 pounds (26 kg) and cost about $100,000. The suits were designed to withstand temperatures ranging from $+230°F$ $(+110°C)$ to $-250°F$ $(-157°C)$.

Apollo 7 was referred to as a ten-day shakedown mission to make sure all of the "bugs" had been worked out of the system. During this mission, all the astronauts had caught colds—this allowed the press to refer to *Apollo 7* as a "ten-day cold capsule." Because of his cold and for other reasons, Wally Schirra became a bit irritable. He refused to make a live TV transmission to the earth until some onboard technical problems were ironed out.

Later, a more genial Schirra made the TV transmissions while the Apollo capsule was traveling over NASA tracking stations in Corpus Christi, Texas, and Cape Canaveral. The *Apollo 7* crew opened their seven-to-eleven-minute telecasts with an irreverent reference to the old radio ballroom broadcasts: "Hello from the lovely Apollo Room, high atop everything. . . ." Their broadcasts were known at NASA as the *Wally, Walt,*

and Donn Show. The crew would eventually win a special Emmy Award for their broadcasts from space.[1]

Even as the mission was drawing to a close, the crew still had colds. Because of this, Wally Schirra thought that wearing helmets on reentry would be unwise, but Mission Control ordered the astronauts to wear their helmets for reentry anyway. Schirra persisted, however, and eventually won out, and all helmets were off when *Apollo 7* splashed down on October 21, 1968.

SCHIRRA AFTER NASA

In 1969, Wally Schirra retired from the U.S. Navy and from the astronaut corps as well. He entered the world of private industry as the president of Regency Investors, Inc., a company that specialized in the international leasing of oil completion facilities, jet transport aircraft, and other high-technology services. Wally Schirra has served as a director or on the boards of directors of a number of high-tech businesses. In January 1979, Wally Schirra became president of Schirra Enterprises.

The crew of Apollo 7 *(left to right): Walt Cunningham, Donn Eisele, Wally Schirra*

PROJECT APOLLO

Project Apollo was initiated in 1960 by President Dwight Eisenhower. His successor, John Kennedy, pledged that Americans would set foot on the moon by the end of the 1960s. During the years of the Mercury and Gemini programs, Apollo planners were debating the vehicles and the methods they had to use to reach the moon.

The Apollo capsule held three astronauts and would be carried into orbit by the *Saturn 1B* and ultimately the mammoth *Saturn V* rocket.

NASA was full of confidence from their triumphant Mercury and Gemini missions, but the end of the decade was drawing nearer and nearer. The American astronauts wanted desperately to fulfill Kennedy's pledge. To the discouragement and despair of the nation, the Apollo program would begin tragically.

THE *APOLLO 1* FIRE

Ed White, Gus Grissom, and Roger Chaffee were selected to be the *Apollo 1* astronauts. On January 27, 1967, the *Apollo 1* capsule was to undergo a routine electricity test, switching from externally supplied electricity that was coming from the Space Center, to internal power that came from batteries aboard the craft. The simple test had taken much longer than usual because of a problem communicating with those in the flight control building. At 6:30 P.M. a sharp power surge went through the craft, then disappeared as quickly as it came. But at 6:31, cries of "Hey!" and "Fire!" were heard. One second later, sensors showed the cabin temperature rising dangerously. Many believe it was Ed White who called out, "Fire in the cockpit." Other garbled and terrifying words were uttered by the doomed astronauts. The last words that came from the burning capsule were "Fire in the spacecraft!" It took less than thirty seconds for the men to lose consciousness and perish in the blaze. Their official cause of death was given as asphyxiation due to smoke inhalation.

Gus Grissom is reported to have had some doubts about the reliability of the first Apollo spacecrafts and is quoted as having said that his complaints weren't paid enough attention. "I've been howling in the wilderness for years," he said, according to *The Space Program Quiz and Fact Book.*

The *Apollo 1* tragedy was believed to have been caused by a bundle of wires under Grissom's couch that had short-circuited when their Teflon insulation was scraped away by the metal edge of a waste-disposal-unit door. The sparks from the wires started a fire in a spacecraft filled with pure oxygen, in whose presence other materials become highly combustible. Many flammable plastics were used in the Apollo cabin, including nylon netting that was slung under the crew's couches. These synthetics contributed decisively to the fire.[1] The capsule wasn't even equipped with a fire extinguisher. The crew's final means of survival, the escape hatch, took too long to open—it would have taken ninety seconds to open under the very best of circumstances.

THE SATURN V BOOSTER

The *Saturn V* was, and to date still is, the biggest rocket ever made. With the Apollo command and service modules attached, it stands four times taller than the Redstone that shot Alan Shepard's Mercury capsule into space in 1961. As with most powerful rockets, the Saturn V came in multiple stages, with each stage giving an extra "push" to the crew cabin, sending it into orbit.

The first stage of the *Saturn V* was 138 feet (42 m) tall and over 30 feet (9 m) across. This stage contained over 500,000 gallons (1.9 million liters) of liquid oxygen, which combined with kerosene to propel the rocket. There were five 18-foot (5.5-m) -tall rocket engines at the base of the *Saturn V,* which consumed 700 tons of fuel per minute. In their two-and-a-half-minute flight, the five engines generated 7.5 million pounds (3.4 million kg) of *thrust*—blasting an Apollo team 38 miles (61 km) into the atmosphere at speeds up to 6,100 miles (9,800 km) per hour.

When the fuel from the first stage was depleted, its hollow aluminum shell would drop away into the ocean. The second stage of the *Saturn V* booster was 81 feet (24.7 m) tall and the two tanks within its casing held 350,000 gallons (1.3 million liters) of liquid oxygen and liquid hydrogen. Like the first stage, the second had five rocket engines that generated over 1 million pounds (about 1/2 million kg) of thrust, boosting the Apollo craft into *near* orbit and increasing its speed to over 15,000 miles (24,000 km) per hour.

The third and final stage of the *Saturn V* rocket was 58 feet (17.7 m) tall. It had only *one* engine of the same type as the five that propelled the second stage. The third stage was fueled by over 80,000 gallons (303,000 liters) of liquid hydrogen, which combined with liquid oxygen. When this one engine fired in near orbit (in very little gravity compared to that on earth), the single engine would boost the command and service modules to a speed of 17,400 miles (28,000 km) per hour. On lunar missions, this rocket engine would fire again to set the Apollo craft on the 200,000-mile (322,000-km) voyage to the moon.

THE APOLLO MODULES

Command Module

The cone-shaped command module—about the size of a standard station wagon—is where the astronauts lived and worked in the Apollo craft. Designed by NASA and North American Aviation, the command module was over 10 feet (3 m) high and 12 feet (3.7 m) across at the base of the cone. Inside, the CM was divided into a forward, or crew, compartment and an aft compartment. In the aft compartment were three couches in a row for the three astronauts, and two sleeping bags were slung under the left- and right-hand couches. Only two astronauts were expected to be asleep at a time. The center couch could be folded up, and if this was done there was room enough in the Apollo capsule for two astronauts to stand up (although weightlessness prevented them from standing still). Unlike the Mercury capsule, which had one small porthole, the Apollo craft had five windows for the crew to observe the scenery around them. At the tip of the Apollo's nose cone was the tunnel through which two astronauts would enter the lunar module for their trip to the moon's surface. The tough outer shell of the command module was made of aluminum, and the heat shield was made of stainless steel with phenolic epoxy resin.

Service Module

The service module contained the fuel for the engines as well as the water and oxygen vital to the trip. The service module supported the lives of the

The Apollo craft were more complex than in any previous missions. In this photo taken from Apollo 7's lunar module, David Scott climbs out of the command module. The earth is in the background.

astronauts on the long voyage to and from the moon. It had a single controllable rocket which could generate over 20,000 pounds (9,000 kg) of thrust—this rocket was vital when the time came for the command and service modules to break out of lunar orbit and head for earth. The service module also contained sixteen small rockets to alter the craft's speed and direction. The service module would be discarded before the command module reentered the earth's atmosphere. The service module would burn up before it could hit anything on earth.

Lunar Module

The first moonship in history was manufactured by the Grumman Corporation, which had been working on lunar-landing designs since the early sixties, not long after it had learned of NASA's decision to attempt to land astronauts on the moon. The *lunar module*, or LM (pronounced "lem"), was divided into two parts, the descent stage and the ascent stage.

Constructed of a lightweight aluminum alloy, the descent stage was nearly 30 feet (9 m) across and stood on four spidery legs, specially constructed to touch down evenly when landing on the surface of the moon. The descent stage was powered by a liquid-fueled rocket that generated 10,000 pounds (4,500 kg) of thrust and could be controlled with a throttle. The descent engine handled so easily that the astronauts could actually hover over the lunar surface if they wanted to. In order to fly the LM, the jet-pilot astronauts had to be qualified as helicopter pilots as well. The descent stage also housed most of the crew's life-supporting oxygen and the equipment for scientific experiments.

The ascent stage, the upper part of the LM, contained the crew cabin and the rocket that would propel the LM off the lunar surface and into a rendezvous with the moon-orbiting command module. The ascent rocket generated 3,500 pounds (1,600 kg) of thrust—more than enough to overcome the feeble pull of lunar gravity on such a lightweight craft.

The LM interior comprised the crew compartment, midsection, and equipment bay. The LM wasn't built for comfort—there were no seats or couches, but the moon's gravity being only one-sixth that of earth's, the astronauts could be expected to sleep standing up. The midsection also had a place to store the moon rocks they would bring back to earth. Each of the two astronauts in the LM had one triangular window he could look out of, angled downward so he could get a better view of the landing site during descent.

The craft was too flimsy to either leave or reenter the earth's atmosphere—it was a disposable, outer-space-only type of craft. The outer skin of the LM was not much thicker than heavy-duty aluminum foil. Of course, the LM was built to be used only in space and on the moon, where the gravity is weak, and this fact allowed the LM designers to keep the overall weight of the craft low. The ladder on the LM's landing gear, which the astronauts used to descend to the moon's surface, could only work in lunar gravity. Back on earth, where an astronaut would weigh six times as much as on the moon, the ladder would be too weak to support his weight.

THE PRELUNAR
APOLLO MISSIONS

On October 11, 1968, the stalled Apollo program, due to the *Apollo 1* tragedy, got under way with *Apollo 7*, the first flight test of the new command and service modules in orbit around the earth. Flown by astronauts Wally Schirra, Walt Cunningham, and Donn Eisele, *Apollo 7* also successfully tested the new Apollo spacesuits, which had been redesigned after the *Apollo 1* disaster.

Apollo 8, with Frank Borman, Jim Lovell, and Bill Anders aboard, was the first manned Apollo craft to be launched by the new *Saturn V* rocket, the largest booster ever used in space flight. *Apollo 8* didn't use a lunar module, but NASA engineers put what they called a lunar test article, which weighed the same as the LM, in its place to be sure the Saturn V could lift all the vehicles needed for a moon mission.

The *Saturn V* pushed the command and service modules of *Apollo 8* all the way into lunar orbit, over 200,000 miles (322,000 km) away. This was the first time man had torn free of the gravitational pull of the earth and circled around the far side of the moon. Anders wryly told Mission Control, "The moon isn't made of green cheese at all. It's American cheese!" There was some tension in the mission, for breaking out of lunar orbit required a firing of the service module engine. If the engine failed, *Apollo 8* would orbit the moon forever, with no chance of returning home. On Christmas Eve 1968, *Apollo 8* took one final swing around the moon. Its engine fired up beautifully, and the astronauts were homeward bound. A much relieved Jim Lovell radioed back to earth, "Please be informed, there *is* a Santa Claus."

The flight of *Apollo 9* was the first manned test of a lunar module in earth orbit. Astronauts Jim McDivitt and Russell Schweikert boarded the lunar module *Spider* and undocked from the command module *Gumdrop* with David Scott. This flight proved that the Apollo LM could successfully fly on its own and dock with the command module. These procedures were crucial for lunar missions, which were not very far away after the lunar module *Spider* had proven itself spaceworthy.

The *Apollo 10* astronauts were Tom Stafford, John Young, and Gene

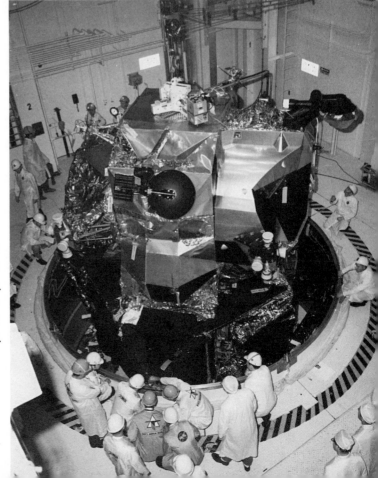

Above: Apollo 9 *command module* Gumdrop *is hoisted aboard a recovery ship.* Right: *the lunar module* Snoopy *is readied for flight aboard* Apollo 10.

Cernan. Their mission was the first test of the lunar module *Snoopy* in lunar orbit, flying just as it would have to in a lunar mission. The LM descended to within 50,000 feet (15,240 m) of the lunar surface—closer than anyone had ever been before. The *Snoopy* then returned to dock with the command module *Charlie Brown* in higher orbit, and the remated vehicles left lunar orbit nose-to-nose for the long trip back to earth. Another objective of the *Apollo 10* mission was to photograph the moon's Sea of Tranquillity, where *Apollo 11* was scheduled to land in July 1969, and to study the effects of the moon's weak and often irregular gravitational field. *Apollo 10* made a total of thirty-one orbits around the moon and splashed down safely on May 26, 1969.

An important discovery was made by the crew of *Apollo 10*—they were the first astronauts to shave in space. There had been a lot of worry at NASA about the possibility of tiny bits of beard stubble floating around the capsule and working its way into the equipment. After many high-tech solutions had been proposed to solve the shaving dilemma, the astronauts finally decided to take matters into their own hands. John Young told Mission Control, "We're in the process now of commencing scientific experiment Sugar Hotel Alpha Victor Echo. And it's going to be conducted like all normal human beings do it." The astronauts used a kind of brushless shave cream available in any drugstore. The whiskers stuck to the cream. No space-age solutions were needed.

THE FLIGHT OF
APOLLO 11

The flight of *Apollo 11*, the first manned mission to the moon, began on July 16, 1969. Under the guidance of astronauts Neil Armstrong, Buzz Aldrin, and Michael Collins, the greatest goal in space flight was achieved—man walked on the moon. The details of this epochal flight are told in the story of Neil Armstrong, commander of the *Apollo 11* mission.

THE POSTLUNAR
APOLLO MISSIONS

America's second mission to the moon, *Apollo 12*, was flown by astronauts Charles Conrad, Richard Gordon, and Alan Bean. While Gordon orbited the moon in the command module *Yankee Clipper*, Conrad and Bean piloted the lunar module *Intrepid* into the Oceanus Procellarum region of the moon. The unmanned moon probe *Surveyor 3* had landed there two and one half years before. (The first "frisbee" game on the moon was played by Alan Bean and Charles Conrad of *Apollo 12*. The flying disk, which floated along smoothly in the weak lunar gravity, was actually a canister lid.)

Conrad and Bean conducted more experiments on the lunar surface before blasting off the moon and into rendezvous with the *Yankee Clipper*. The *Apollo 12* capsule splashed down in the Pacific on November 24, 1969, after a flawless ten-day mission.

When Apollo astronauts returned from the moon, they were kept in a quarantine trailer for the first eighteen days they spent back on earth. NASA doctors were worried that the astronauts might have brought back a bacteria that was unknown on earth and uncontrollable.

During the *Apollo 12* mission, Conrad and Bean actually *did* come across the first living organism discovered outside of the earth. In the foam insulation surrounding *Surveyor 3*'s TV camera, scientists discovered a living colony of bacteria.

This was no plague from space, but the common earth germ *Streptococcus mitis*, which had been transported to the moon via *Surveyor 3* a few years before, and which had survived for years in the airless lunar environment. The plots of the science-fiction movies *The War of the Worlds* and *The First Men in the Moon* both hinged upon creatures from outer space being killed off by a common earth germ.

Eventually, NASA doctors became certain that no alien germs were coming back with the astronauts, and the crew of *Apollo 14* were the last astronauts quarantined after returning from the moon.

THE *APOLLO 13* EXPLOSION

A group of engineers from Mission Control had put a telescope on a high Houston rooftop and were recording a visual tracking of *Apollo 13* with a TV camera as the spacecraft orbited the moon. All of a sudden, a glowing circle of light appeared where the craft should have been on their monitors. On board *Apollo 13*, two explosions had ripped through the liquid oxygen tanks in the service module.

"Houston, we seem to have a problem," came a message from John Swigert of *Apollo 13* on April 13, 1970. Swigert and crewmates Jim Lovell and Fred Haise were rapidly losing power and oxygen in the command module *Odyssey*. Much of the service module had been destroyed or damaged in the explosion, and the crew was 205,000 miles (330,000 km) from home. The craft now wobbled disturbingly in flight. With the command module about to lose all power in fifteen minutes, they climbed aboard the lunar module *Aquarius*. They were forced to use the LM as a lifeboat for most of the trip and then enter the command module for reentry into earth's atmosphere. The LM wasn't designed to be used this way—and it was only built to carry two. The crew took water into the LM in plastic bottles and improvised other life-support systems where they could. In trouble and very, very far from home, Haise, Lovell, and Swigert crowded into the *Aquarius* and made the best of it.

What *Apollo 13* had to do was use the gravitational pull of the moon to "slingshot" them back toward the earth in a severely damaged craft. By the time the astronauts returned to earth, they were tired and dehydrated. Days of fatigue were making the crew mistake-prone, but ground controllers tried to keep the flight on an even keel. *Apollo 13*'s approach to the atmosphere looked too shallow—they very nearly skipped off into space. Yet they successfully splashed down, and the grateful astronauts were picked up by the aircraft carrier *Iwo Jima*.

Alan Shepard, Stuart Roosa, and Edgar Mitchell were the crew of *Apollo 14*. While Roosa orbited the moon in the *Kitty Hawk*, Shepard and Mitchell descended in the LM *Antares*, which landed in the Fra Mauro region (where *Apollo 13* was supposed to have set down). For the first time, the lunar module carried a large piece of equipment to the moon— the wheelbarrowlike mobile equipment transporter. Also, photographs were taken for possible future landing sites on the moon.

The first extrasensory perception (ESP) experiments were conducted by Edgar Mitchell aboard *Apollo 14*. By a previous agreement with four earthbound psychics back in the United States, Mitchell would concentrate on each card in a deck of twenty-five that were marked with the special symbols used in ESP experiments. At several appointed times, the psychics would try to "receive" Mitchell's thought waves that would tell them the correct order of the cards. Perhaps brainwaves burn up in reentry, because the number of cards they'd named correctly was scarcely better than if they had picked the cards at random.

Launched on July 26, 1971, *Apollo 15* took astronauts David Scott and Jim Irwin to the moon in the lunar module *Falcon*, which landed in the Hadley Rille area. Alfred Worden kept his orbiting vigil aboard the command module *Endeavor*. The lunar activity of *Apollo 15* marked the first use of the lunar roving vehicle (LRV), usually called the Lunar Rover. Looking like a stripped-down dune buggy, the lunar rover was about 10 feet (3 m) long and 6 feet 9 inches (2.1 m) wide. Each wheel was individually powered, and its top speed was 8.7 miles (14 km). The LRV was used to explore the mountainous Hadley Apennine region of the moon.

As a tribute to the American astronauts and the Soviet cosmonauts who died in the race to land on the moon, the crew of *Apollo 15* left on the lunar surface a small aluminum sculpture called "The Fallen Astronaut," by Paul Van Hoeydonck. Next to it was a plaque naming the four-

Jim Irwin salutes the American flag he planted outside the Apollo 15 module.

*The commemorative plaque stuck in the lunar
soil by David Scott and Jim Irwin*

teen spacemen of East and West who gave their lives for space exploration.

With a crew of veteran astronaut John Young and rookies Tom Mattingly and Charles Duke, *Apollo 16* left earth for the moon on April 16, 1972. While Mattingly kept the command module *Caspar* in steady lunar orbit, Young and Duke took the LM *Orion* into the Descartes region of the moon, near the North Ray crater. Young and Duke also used the LRV to explore the lunar highlands. The mission of *Apollo 16* was the first use of the moon as an astronomical observatory.

The final Apollo mission to the moon started with the firing of *Apollo 17*'s *Saturn V* booster on December 7, 1972. The mission was commanded by Gene Cernan, who with Harrison Schmitt, landed the lunar module *Challenger* safely in the Taurus-Littrow area of the moon. While Ronald Evans circled above in the command module *America*, Cernan and Schmitt set a record for longest time of any lunar mission, as well as bringing back the most lunar samples of any mission. Cernan and Schmitt also drove the last LRV on a moon mission.

The last words spoken on the moon were uttered by Gene Cernan. They were: "We leave now as we once came, with peace and with hope for all mankind." With that, the *Challenger* blasted off from the lunar surface and returned to orbit with the *America*. The last set of lunarnauts splashed down on earth on December 19, 1972.

SKYLAB

Upon conclusion of the Apollo lunar exploration program, the Skylab program began. *Skylab 1* was launched on May 14, 1973. It was an unmanned launch, containing the OWS, the orbiting workshop that the Skylab astronauts would inhabit during their weeks in orbit. It was a cylinder, about the size of a small house. The upper part of the OWS was the experiment chamber. The lower part contained a galley, bathroom, sleeping compartments, work areas, and storage areas. The zero-gravity shower sent water in all directions, but the astronauts got clean nonetheless. Food on *Skylab* was far better than anything NASA had concocted up to that point, with such delicacies as filet mignon and lobster Newburg on the menu.

Skylab had two sets of solar energy panels that would give the ship its power. There were two broad winglike panels on the side of the crew compartment and a windmill-like arrangement of four wings that surrounded the Apollo telescope mount.

Unfortunately, the OWS was damaged during launch, and a crew of astronauts had to get up there as soon as possible to try to correct the problem. The crew of *Skylab 2* left earth on May 25, 1973. They were Charles Conrad, Joseph Kerwin, and Paul Weitz. In orbit for about a month, the crew repaired the ailing OWS as well as performed valuable experiments on the effects of long-term space flight. They also did experiments in earth resources and solar astronomy using the 10-ton Apollo telescope mount.

Skylab 3 was launched on July 28, 1973. Medical, *astrophysics*, and more earth resources experiments were performed by astronauts Alan Bean, Owen Garriott, and Jack Lousma. They worked in orbit for about two months before splashing down on September 25, 1973.

Skylab 4 was launched on November 16, 1973, for a mission that would last eighty-four days, one hour, and sixteen minutes. Crewmen Gerald Carr, Edward Gibson, and William Pogue completed a total of fifty-eight experiments in the areas of biomedicine, solar astronomy, solar physics, and engineering. They even observed the newly discovered Comet Kohoutek.

On *Skylab 3*, an event took place that was of greater importance than even the first shave in space: the first haircut in space. Owen Garriott was the barber who cut Alan Bean's hair, while Bean chased after the weightless clippings with a suction tube.

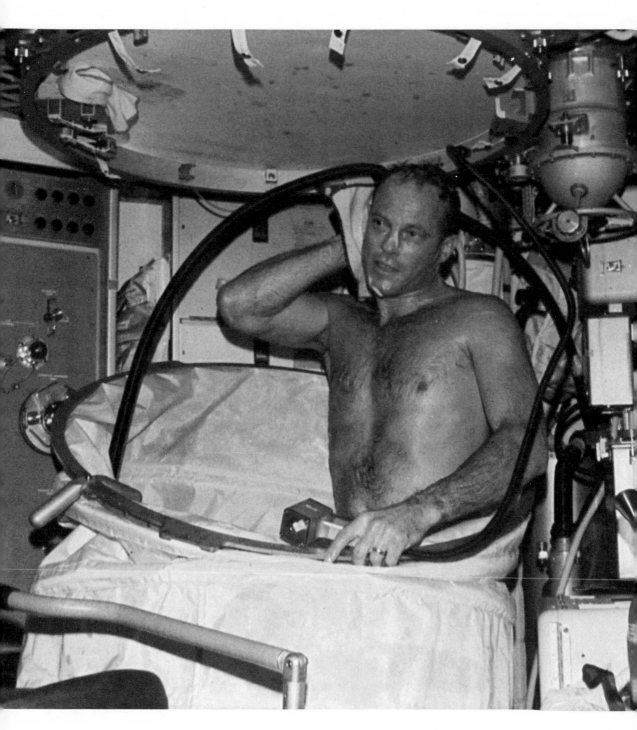

Jack Lousma taking a hot bath aboard Skylab 3

THE APOLLO MISSIONS

No.	Astronauts	Craft Names	Launched
7	Wally Schirra, Donn Eisele, Walt Cunningham	———	October 11, 1968
8	Frank Borman, Jim Lovell, William Anders	———	December 21, 1968
9	Jim McDivitt, David Scott, Russ Schweickert	*Gumdrop* and *Spider*	March 3, 1969
10	Thomas Stafford, John Young, Gene Cernan	*Charlie Brown* and *Snoopy*	May 18, 1969
11	Neil Armstrong, Michael Collins, Buzz Aldrin	*Columbia* and *Eagle*	July 16, 1969
12	Charles Conrad, Richard Gordon, Alan Bean	*Yankee Clipper* and *Intrepid*	November 14, 1969
13	Jim Lovell, John Swigert, Fred Haise	*Odyssey* and *Aquarius*	April 11, 1970
14	Alan Shepard, Stuart Roosa, Edgar Mitchell	*Kitty Hawk* and *Antares*	January 31, 1971
15	David Scott, Alfred Worden, Jim Irwin	*Endeavor* and *Falcon*	July 26, 1971
16	John Young, Tom Mattingly, Charles Duke	*Caspar* and *Orion*	April 16, 1972
17	Gene Cernan, Ronald Evans, Harrison Schmitt	*America* and *Challenger*	December 7, 1972

SKYLAB MISSIONS

No.	Astronauts	Launched
2	Charles Conrad, Joseph Kerwin, and Paul Weitz	May 25, 1973
3	Alan Bean, Owen Garriott, and Jack Lousma	July 28, 1973
4	Gerald Carr, Edward Gibson, and William Pogue	November 16, 1973

The crew of *Skylab 4* accomplished a much tougher first, though. They stayed in earth orbit from November 16, 1973, to February 8, 1974. At one point during their eighty-four-day marathon mission, they once called a (brief) strike to protest the busy schedule Houston expected them to stick to every day.

Five years after Carr, Gibson, and Pogue left the vacant *Skylab* orbiting the earth, NASA scientists knew that its orbit was decaying rapidly and would probably fall to earth sometime in the summer of 1979. There was some hope that the space shuttle could be used to save *Skylab*, but the shuttle wasn't operational yet.

What made *Skylab*'s decaying orbit so newsworthy was that pieces of the craft were expected to be too large to burn up upon reentry into the earth's atmosphere. People everywhere wondered literally *where* in the world the 85-ton *Skylab* would fall and what damage it might do. Although some final adjustments were made to its orbit directing it over less populated areas, there was little else the world could do but watch and wait. When *Skylab* finally crashed, most of it landed in the South Pacific and Indian oceans. One part *did* crash to the ground, landing on July 11, 1979, in sparsely inhabited western Australia. The only reported death was an unlucky jackrabbit that was beaned by an oxygen tank.

THE LAST APOLLO FLIGHT

The final mission of the Apollo program was the Apollo-Soyuz test project, which was manned by Tom Stafford, Vance Brand, and Deke Slayton. The

APOLLO-SOYUZ TEST PROJECT

Astronauts	*Launched*
U.S.A.: Thomas Stafford, Vance Brand, and Deke Slayton	July 15, 1975
USSR: Alexei Leonov and Valery Kubasov	

Apollo craft would rendezvous and dock in earth orbit with the cosmonauts Alexei Leonov and Valery Kubasov aboard *Soyuz 19*. The details of this unusual and historic flight are included in the story of Deke Slayton. The Apollo-Soyuz Test Project was the last time an Apollo vehicle would orbit the earth.

NEIL A. ARMSTRONG
First to Walk on
the Moon

More than any other astronaut, Neil Armstrong characterizes the American space program. A top-notch pilot, he would prove himself an astronaut among astronauts in a real outer-space emergency. Then, with quiet courage and dignity, Neil Armstrong thrilled the world by perfectly completing the greatest voyage in history—the flight to the moon.

THE AIRSTRIP GREASEMONKEY

Neil Armstrong was born 6 miles (10 km) outside of Wapakoneta, Ohio, in the living room of his grandparents' farmhouse, on August 5, 1930. Neil's father, Steven Armstrong, was employed by the state of Ohio. His mother, Viola Engel Armstrong, had a strong interest in literature and music. (The Armstrongs were to have two more boys after Neil.)

Neil read ninety books during his first-grade year and skipped the second grade altogether because tests showed his reading to be on a fifth-grade level. He would spend much of his early years playing the baritone horn and piano, participating in the Boy Scouts, and looking at the heavens through a neighbor's small telescope.

At only age six, Neil flew for the first time. His father took him aloft in a Ford trimotor plane. Before long, Neil's room was filled with model airplanes, and he even began picking up work at the local airport. It was only

The crew of Apollo 11 (left to right):
Neil Armstrong, Michael Collins, Edwin Aldrin

a matter of time before Neil Armstrong had his pilot's license—even before he got his driver's license.

Neil's father had a job that kept him moving from one Ohio town to another. The family had moved six times by the time Neil was six years old. Neil's first job came when he was seven, cutting grass at a local cemetery for ten cents an hour. Years later, he worked as a drugstore stockboy in the town of Wapakoneta. In high school, Neil did well in math and science. He was so far advanced in his studies that he even taught a class for his fellow students when the teacher was out sick!

Neil attended Purdue University, working toward a bachelor's degree in aeronautical engineering, but he left school after two years to fly combat missions for the Navy during the Korean War. Although he flew seventy-eight combat missions from the aircraft carrier U.S.S. *Essex*, Neil was the youngest pilot in the squadron. On one bombing run, he lost one of the wings of his jet, but still managed to keep the crippled plane in the air until he'd left enemy territory. He succeeded in bailing out over friendlier surroundings.

He returned to Purdue after his military service and received his bachelor's degree. Later he earned a master of science degree in aerospace engineering from the University of Southern California.

Armstrong then joined the National Advisory Committee on Aeronautics, which would become NASA. Neil, his wife Janet, and two sons, Mark and Richard, moved to southern California, where Neil worked as a civilian test pilot at Edwards Air Force Base. During this period, their daughter Karen died tragically of a brain tumor.

Neil's hobbies include fishing and listening to a variety of music. A very reclusive man, he prefers to remain out of the public eye.

GEMINI 8

Before joining the astronaut corps, Neil Armstrong flew the experimental rocket plane the X-15. It was considered one of the ultimate challenges for a test pilot. He was also involved with the experimental Dynamic Soaring of Dyna-Soar project. Both X-15 and Dyna-Soar aircraft could be considered forerunners of the space shuttle—spacecraft that could land like aircraft.

Neil Armstrong's first mission was the *Gemini 8* flight with David Scott. Launched on March 16, 1966, the principal mission of *Gemini 8* was the first docking with an unmanned spacecraft in earth orbit. An Agena rocket was sent into orbit for the rendezvous and docking.

After the rendezvous with the Agena vehicle, Armstrong radioed to Mission Control: "Okay, just for your information, the Agena was very stable and at the present time we're having no noticeable oscillations at all."

About a half-hour later, the mission would present the first emergency to strike an American spacecraft in orbit.

Armstrong and Scott were still docked with the orbiting Agena rocket when a Gemini thruster malfunctioned. The two vehicles started spinning around each other. The astronauts cut the Gemini capsule free from the Agena, but the spinning continued. Armstrong radioed Mission Control, "We're backing off. . . . We've got serious problems here. . . . We're tumbling end over end . . . and we can't turn anything off!" The spacecraft cartwheeled wildly through space, in grave danger of striking the Agena. The intense centrifugal force made it extremely difficult to operate the controls, but Armstrong gradually brought the capsule back on an even keel. Unfortunately, they had used up most of their fuel, but about halfway through their seventh orbit, the craft was stabilized. Later, it was determined that the spinning was caused by a short circuit that made one thruster fire continuously.

"We felt something that Dave was to describe later as a case of 'constructive alarm,' " Armstrong told *Life*. "We were darned well aware of a serious emergency, but were instantly preoccupied with how to get out of it. . . . We never once doubted we would find an answer—but we had to find it fast. . . . The sun flashed through the window about once a second. The sensations were much like those you would feel during an aircraft spin. Neither of us felt the approach of losing consciousness, but if the rates continued to increase we knew an intolerable level would be reached."

Thankful for a happy outcome to the first full-fledged emergency in orbit, the *Gemini 8* crew cut their mission short and headed directly for home.

THE FLIGHT OF *APOLLO 11*

To prepare for a lunar flight and landing, each of the *Apollo 11* astronauts had to spend at least 400 hours in *simulators* of the command and lunar modules. Since before the training began, Neil Armstrong knew he was the right man to command the first voyage to the moon. "I have been in relatively high-risk businesses all my adult life," Neil Armstrong remarked to *Life*. "Few of the others, however, had the possibility of direct gains in knowledge which this one has. I have confidence in the equipment, the planning, the training."

Apollo 11 *lifts off on July 16, 1969.*

The launch of *Apollo 11* occurred at 9:32 in the morning on July 16, 1969, from pad 39-A at the Kennedy Space Center. For the first four days of the mission, Armstrong, Aldrin, and Collins did little that was history-making. They kept all systems in check for the lunar orbit and landing, did what assignments Houston sent them, and regularly sent live TV broadcasts back to a curious earth.

At the same time as the *Apollo 11* flight, the Soviet Union had sent up an unmanned moon-probe called *Luna 15*. As signees of the United Nations Outer Space Treaty of 1967, American and Soviet space agencies would notify each other to prevent the mission of one country from interfering with the mission of another. Two days after launch, astronaut Frank Borman contacted the Soviets and was reassured by the president of the Soviet Academy of Sciences that *Luna 15* would not get in the way of *Apollo 11*. (It is widely believed that *Luna 15* crashed into the moon during the *Apollo 11* mission.)[1]

After the successful linkup of the *Columbia* and *Eagle* modules, the next difficult moment of the *Apollo 11* flight was the transition to lunar orbit. The Apollo craft would fire a rocket to slow itself down enough for the moon's gravity to grab hold of it in orbit. If the rocket was too weak, the astronauts would simply head straight for home; if it fired too powerfully, they would crash into the lunar surface. The astronauts swung around the far side of the moon, where all radio contact would be lost. While ground controllers in Houston hoped for the best, the *Apollo* fired its single rocket engine, and a stable lunar orbit was established.

After *Apollo*'s thirteenth orbit of the moon, the LM was separated from the command module and started on its 50,000-foot (15,200-m) descent to the Sea of Tranquillity. (Located along the lunar equator, the Sea of Tranquillity was an easier spot for a landing than nonequatorial areas.) "The *Eagle* has wings," Armstrong told Mike Collins as the LM began its graceful 300-mile (480-km) arc downward to the moon's surface. By the time the LM had dropped down to 7,200 feet (2,200 m), they were 5 miles (8 km) from the projected landing site. When the small lunar module was hovering about 300 feet (90 m) above the landing site, both astronauts knew that they couldn't land as planned. The terrain was strewn with boulders. Hitting a boulder could have caused the LM to tip over or break its landing gear, and Armstrong and Aldrin would have been stranded on the moon for all time. "The auto-targeting was taking us right into a football [-field] -sized crater, with a large number of boulders and rocks," they radioed back. The *Eagle* kept looking for a suitable landing site, but the fuel supply was nearly depleted. If a landing couldn't be made in a few moments, Armstrong and Aldrin would have to fire the ascent rocket and return to the ship. Finally, Armstrong found an acceptable spot. "Houston," came Armstrong's words from the moon, "Tranquillity Base here. The *Eagle* has landed."

MEN ON THE MOON

The *Apollo 11* lunar team felt so energetic after touching down on the moon, they requested to go outside a few hours earlier than scheduled. CapCom Deke Slayton in Houston said it was okay, so the astronauts suited up and prepared to set foot on the moon for the first time in human history. It took longer than expected to depressurize the *Eagle*, but eventually the oxygen was out of it and the astronauts could open the hatch. As Neil Armstrong told Houston when he stood on what was officially known as the "egress platform": "Okay, Houston. I'm on the porch."

When Neil Armstrong set foot on the moon, the historic words recorded were, "That's one small step for man; one giant leap for mankind." But in the long trip from the moon to earth, it seems a word may have been lost in Armstrong's famous utterance. What many believe Armstrong really said was, "That's one small step for *a* man; one giant leap for mankind." Radio static could have made the short syllable "a" inaudible and forever altered what has to be one of the most famous sentences ever spoken.

Armstrong and Aldrin carried with them a small piece of the propeller and a scrap of the original fabric from the Wright brothers' first plane, the *Kitty Hawk*.

Neil Armstrong described the lunar surface to the watching world: "The surface is fine and powdery. I can pick it up loosely with my toe. It does adhere in fine layers like powdered charcoal to the sole and sides of my boots. I only go in a small fraction of an inch, maybe an eighth of an inch. But I can see the footprints of my boots and the treads in the fine sandy particles."

The spacesuits, which had been so confining in earthbound rehearsals, now weighed only one-sixth their true weight of 185 pounds (84 kg). Armstrong and Aldrin found walking in the suits refreshingly easy. Their first task was to collect a "contingency sample" in case the mission had to be aborted. Then they inspected the LM for damage it may have suffered in descent. They found the LM to be in perfect shape, and at that point President Richard Nixon called to congratulate them. "Because of what you have done, the heavens have become a part of man's world," he told the astronauts, who stood attentively in front of their spacecraft. Once the presidential phone call was over, Armstrong and Aldrin began their moon duties in earnest.

As if cribbing for an exam, each of the moonwalkers had a printed

*Neil Armstrong returns to the
lunar module* Eagle *after
his historic walk on the moon.*

Left: *Armstrong and Aldrin left this plaque on the moon to commemorate their visit.* Below: *Edwin Aldrin heads out for a moonwalk. This photograph was taken by Neil Armstrong.*

checklist on a sleeve of his spacesuit. Their principal tasks were to set up three lunar experiments and to collect rock samples (60 pounds, or 27 kg, was the absolute limit).

The first experiment was designed to attract and provide a sample of the solar winds, which are the flowing of such gases as argon, krypton, xenon, neon, and helium in the solar system.

The next experiment was designed to monitor any seismic activity on the moon. This would not only keep track of any moonquakes or tremors, but would also register any meteors that might hit the moon's crater-pocked surface.

The final experiment involved a laser reflector with dimensions of about 2 feet (0.6 m) square. It would reflect light from earth and allow scientists to get the most precise measurement to date of the distance between the earth and the moon.

After their moonwalk, Neil Armstrong and Buzz Aldrin entered the LM. One of their bulky spacesuits accidentally snapped off the switch that armed the ascent-stage rocket, which would get them off the lunar surface. Houston suggested they improvise with a ball-point pen to control the switch. Fortunately for them, the pen did the trick.

HEADING FOR HOME

The next day, the time had come to rejoin the command module *Columbia* in lunar orbit. Armstrong and Aldrin were fully aware that if the ascent rocket failed to ignite, they would spend their last hours as prisoners of the moon. At 1:55 P.M. on Monday, July 21, the *Eagle*'s ascent rocket fired; three hours and forty minutes later, the *Eagle* made a bumpy but triumphant linkup with the command module *Columbia*, and Armstrong, Aldrin, and Collins started their long flight back to earth.

During the sixty-hour flight back home, *Apollo 11* made live television broadcasts and performed the usual onboard chores of space flight. At 12:22 P.M. on Thursday, July 24, the command module jettisoned the service module and prepared for reentry, hurtling earthward at a speed of 24,000 miles (38,600 km) per hour. After traveling half a million miles (800,000 km), the astronauts reached their splashdown point, 950 miles (1,500 km) southwest of Hawaii. The jubilant *Apollo 11* crew radioed to the aircraft carrier U.S.S. *Hornet*: "All three of us are excellent. Take your time."

While the astronauts were in postflight quarantine, President Nixon visited them on the *Hornet*, where they were kept in isolation for eighteen days. Before their mission to the moon, both Nixon and former Pres-

Eight days after takeoff, the Apollo 11 command module reached its splashdown point and was retrieved by the U.S.S. Hornet.

ident Lyndon Johnson were prevented from having dinner with the astronauts—NASA doctors didn't want the astronauts to risk exposure to any germs, even presidential ones.

AFTER APOLLO

After the international acclaim he received as the first man on the moon, Neil Armstrong slipped intentionally out of public view. He took a job at NASA headquarters in Washington as deputy associate administrator for aeronautics in the Office of Advanced Research and Technology.

Neil Armstrong is currently a professor of aerospace engineering at the University of Cincinnati, where he both teaches and conducts aerospace research.

DONALD K. SLAYTON
First to Dock with
a Foreign Spacecraft

Donald "Deke" Slayton was the Mercury astronaut who didn't enter space until the final Apollo mission. One of the original seven astronauts, Slayton was taken out of commission early in his career. He stood on the sidelines and nearly watched the space program go right past him, but Deke Slayton got a lucky break at the last moment. He participated in an unbelievable mission—an orbital docking between Soviet and American spacecrafts. Deke Slayton, who was present for the starting gun of the space race, now clasped hands with a Russian cosmonaut as a stirring testament to East-West cooperation.

THE NINETEEN-YEAR-OLD
BOMBER PILOT

Donald Kent—otherwise known as "Deke"—Slayton started his long road to space flight in Sparta, Wisconsin, on March 1, 1924. He attended Sparta High School until World War II put every able-bodied young man on notice for military service. Deke entered the Air Force as an aviation cadet and earned his wings after flight training in Texas.

In 1943, Slayton became a B-52 pilot with the 340th Bombardment Group, flying fifty-six combat missions over Europe. After a period in 1944 when he became a B-52 instructor in South Carolina, he returned to com-

bat duty in the Pacific. Slayton was sent to Okinawa with the 319th Bombardment Group, for whom he flew seven combat missions over Japan.

After another brief stint as a B-52 instructor, Slayton left the Air Force to attend the University of Minnesota, where he would get his bachelor of science degree in aeronautical engineering. Slayton immediately found work with the aircraft giant, the Boeing Company, where he stayed for two years. But in 1951, Slayton was called back into active duty with the Minnesota National Guard. He would spend the next four years flying for the Air Force in Minneapolis and West Germany.

In 1955 Deke enrolled in the Air Force Test Pilots School at Edwards Air Force Base in southern California. At around this time, he met and married the former Marjory Lunney. They had a son, Kent, in 1957. Slayton test-piloted fighter aircraft from January 1956 until April 1959.

THE MISSION THAT
NEVER WAS

The Mercury astronauts were introduced in April 1959. That same year, NASA doctors examined Slayton and discovered a heart irregularity. Deke Slayton was originally scheduled to fly the second Mercury orbital mission, but the assignment was passed along to Scott Carpenter. "I got zapped by a three-man board of civilian doctors who didn't examine me except for about two minutes with a stethoscope," he told *Time*. Although the heart problem was discovered three years before, he wasn't grounded until March 1962, agonizingly close to his forfeited Mercury mission.

"I was very upset, to put it mildly," Slayton was quoted in *Spaceflight*. "I thought it was uncalled for; I didn't believe I had a problem. A lot of people that I had a lot of confidence in didn't think I had a problem. . . . I still think it was a lousy decision." Although he could have been bitter, Deke Slayton instead continued to work in the space program as coordinator of astronaut activities. In 1963 he resigned his Air Force commission and became the director of flight crew operations, which put him in charge of almost every area of astronaut training, equipment, and procedure.

The duties of the head of the Astronaut Office can be very lonely at times. After the *Apollo 11* mission, a Texas congressman wanted to give the Congressional Medal of Honor to Neil Armstrong, Buzz Aldrin, and

Air Force Cadet Donald Slayton,
age eighteen, during World War II

Mike Collins. After a great deal of soul-searching on the matter, Deke Slayton told the congressman that the award would be contrary to the spirit of cooperation among the astronauts. Slayton felt that the lunar landing was the result of the efforts of hundreds, not just three individuals. To avoid any conflict or ill will, Congress invented a new medal, the Congressional *Space* Medal of Honor, and presented one to Neil Armstrong.

In the astronaut corps since 1959, Deke Slayton submitted to a heart probe—an angiogram. Slayton's heart was found to be quite healthy. He was finally given back his flight status in March 1972. At the age of forty-eight, he was assigned a flight on *Apollo 18*, the Apollo-Soyuz Test Project—the final Apollo mission. "Man, I tell you, this is worth waiting sixteen years for," he said at the time.

A SUMMIT IN SPACE

The idea of a Soviet-American space mission actually began in the worst days of the space race. At the 1961 Vienna Summit attended by President John Kennedy and Premier Nikita Khrushchev, Kennedy playfully suggested, "Let's go to the moon together." Khrushchev's immediate answer was, "Why not?"[1]

The resulting joint mission would not come to pass for fourteen years, long after the deaths of both Kennedy and Khrushchev. Planning for the cooperative space shot was a nightmare. Whenever technical problems didn't arise, diplomatic ones certainly did. Over whose country would the craft broadcast to earth? Which experiments would each team of astronauts conduct? When the two teams of spacemen met, in whose craft would they shake hands? Who should speak first? In what language? With neither side completely trusting the other, absolute equality had to be maintained at all times. This proved to be difficult on technical matters, where the Soviets have been fanatically security-conscious.

Aside from any cultural barriers, the simple language barrier between Americans and Soviets would have to be dealt with. The Americans would learn Russian, the Russians English. With his Oklahoma drawl, Tom Stafford never failed to crack up cosmonauts Alexei Leonov and Valery Kubasov, who found his "Oklahomski" to be as amusing as it was cryptic. Deke Slayton did his best to learn some basic Russian too. "I can't say that I mastered it," he mentioned to *Science Digest*. "I don't even speak English all that well."

There were some who thought that Deke Slayton should step aside and let a younger astronaut take his place. Slayton himself phrased the question combatively: "What do you mean, I'm too old for orbit; I feel natural out there," he said to *Science Digest*, adding, "Also, I've known men who were old at twenty-five."

"For some people life begins at forty; for me it's going to be more like fifty plus," he told *Time*. At fifty-one, Deke Slayton was the oldest man to fly in space. (The old-age record would eventually be held by Karl Heniec, who flew aboard shuttle mission STS-51F at the age of fifty-eight.)

On July 15, 1975, a Saturn 1B rocket launched the *Apollo 18* craft manned by Deke Slayton, Thomas Stafford, and Vance Brand into orbit. On the same day, the *Soyuz 19* craft bearing cosmonauts Leonov and Kubasov took off from their Central Asian space center near Tyvratum. The Soviet ambassador attended the Apollo launch and the American ambassador attended the Soyuz launch—another diplomatic trade-off.

According to plan, the Soyuz craft orbited the earth first. The far nimbler Apollo craft caught up to the Soyuz on the Soyuz's twenty-ninth orbit. At that point, the two ships linked up, using their new universal docking system.

After successful docking, again as planned, Leonov crawled through the docking module and knocked on the Apollo hatch. At this point, Tom Stafford kiddingly asked, "Who's there?" in Russian. For forty-four hours, the two crews met, laughed, and ate while in earth orbit. Each crew spoke to both President Gerald Ford and to Soviet premier Leonid Brezhnev. The two crews conducted joint scientific experiments and engineering investigations—they even conducted a live press conference from space! There were a great many complaints about the Apollo-Soyuz Test Project (ASTP)—that it was unnecessary, that it cost too much, that the Soviets would greatly benefit from our technology, but we wouldn't learn much from theirs—the list went on and on. Deke Slayton has his own approach to the politics of the ASTP: "Probably the real payoff was in acquiring so many good friends and contacts in the Soviet Union," he told *Science Digest*. "I can't believe that good human contacts like that won't pay off in the long run. I should add that the Russian addiction to secrecy had no bad effects on this mission."

One moment of real danger during the ASTP came on July 24, 1975, when the Apollo craft splashed down. The cone-shaped Apollo command module landed upside-down in the surf, and the cabin quickly filled with poisonous nitrogen tetroxide. Oxygen masks were broken out, but not before Brand had already lost consciousness from the deadly gas. Slayton, Brand, and Stafford all had their lungs blistered before the hatch could be opened. A month later, Deke Slayton underwent surgery to determine if any lasting harm had been done to his lungs. Although the doctors feared that he may have had cancer, the tumor they discovered was benign, or harmless.

Right: Deke Slayton emerges from the Apollo docking module to greet the Soyuz crew. Below: Slayton (right) and Cosmonaut Valeriy Kubasov during a training session at the Johnson Space Center

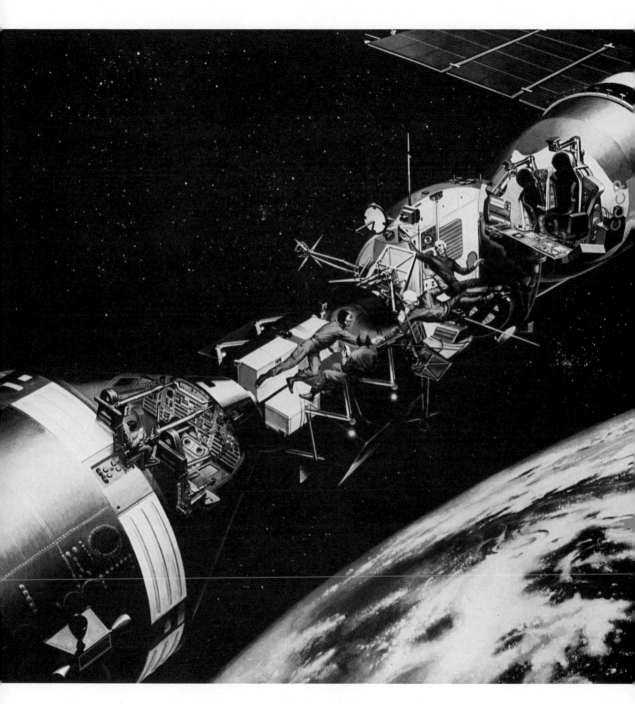

*This artist's concept shows a cutaway view
of the docked Apollo and Soyuz spacecraft*

SLAYTON AND THE SHUTTLE

With his first flight behind him, Deke Slayton logged 217 hours and twenty-eight minutes in space. When asked if he was in any way disappointed by space flight, he told *Science Digest*, "The only big disappointment was coming back down."

After ASTP, Deke Slayton became vitally involved in the early space shuttle testing programs. He had a firm hand in both the Approach and Landing Test as well as the Orbital Flight Test. These were programs of great importance to the success of the shuttle fleet.

Donald K. Slayton retired from NASA on February 27, 1982. Since then he has become a consultant to Aerospace Corporation and chairman of the board of Space Services, Inc.

10

THE SPACE SHUTTLE PROGRAM

The space shuttle is the first orbital spacecraft in history designed to be reusable. Launched like a rocket, it serves as a satellite delivery system and an orbiting laboratory, and provides a multiplicity of other uses. The unique aspect of the shuttle is that it lands like a glider, in shape for repeated later flights. For all the accomplishments of the previous space programs, it didn't matter if their capsules and modules were discarded or recovered; once used, they became museum pieces. The space shuttle program (officially named the Space Transportation System—STS) has paved a sensible and far less costly road into space. With both triumph and tragedy on its record, the space shuttle is the nation's best link to the stars.

THE FIRST ATTEMPTS

The shuttle was *not* the first effort to engineer and fly a reusable spacecraft. There had been several designs for rocket-powered aircraft that would travel in space and land on a runway. Considered the "hottest" of new aircraft designs, these experimental planes were flown by only the top test pilots.

The earliest attempt at a reusable spacecraft was the North American X-15, which was operated jointly by the Air Force and NASA. The X-15 was powered by a rocket, but was launched in flight from another aircraft. The X-15 reached altitudes of 50 miles (80 km) or more, qualifying it as a

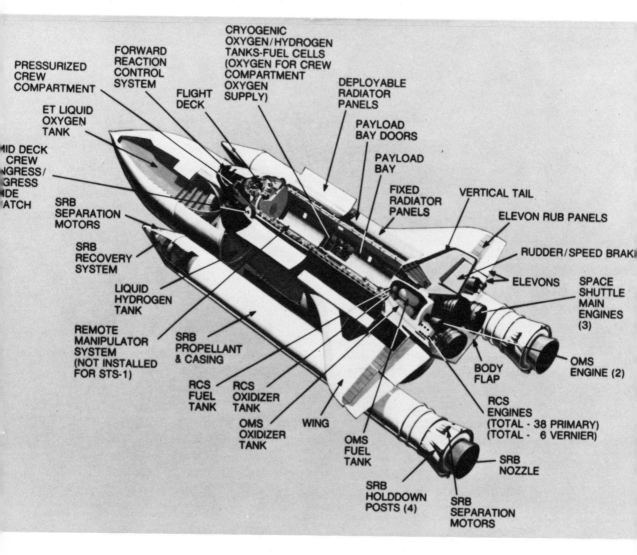

PRESSURIZED CREW COMPARTMENT

FORWARD REACTION CONTROL SYSTEM

CRYOGENIC OXYGEN/HYDROGEN TANKS-FUEL CELLS (OXYGEN FOR CREW COMPARTMENT OXYGEN SUPPLY)

FLIGHT DECK

ET LIQUID OXYGEN TANK

DEPLOYABLE RADIATOR PANELS

PAYLOAD BAY DOORS

PAYLOAD BAY

MID DECK CREW INGRESS/ EGRESS SIDE HATCH

FIXED RADIATOR PANELS

VERTICAL TAIL

SRB SEPARATION MOTORS

ELEVON RUB PANELS

SRB RECOVERY SYSTEM

RUDDER/SPEED BRAKE

ELEVONS

LIQUID HYDROGEN TANK

SPACE SHUTTLE MAIN ENGINES (3)

REMOTE MANIPULATOR SYSTEM (NOT INSTALLED FOR STS-1)

SRB PROPELLANT & CASING

OMS ENGINE (2)

BODY FLAP

RCS FUEL TANK

RCS OXIDIZER TANK

WING

RCS ENGINES (TOTAL - 38 PRIMARY) (TOTAL - 6 VERNIER)

OMS OXIDIZER TANK

OMS FUEL TANK

SRB NOZZLE

SRB HOLDDOWN POSTS (4)

SRB SEPARATION MOTORS

A cutaway view of the space shuttle, shown with payload bays open, reveals the vehicle's major components.

spaceship—although it never entered earth orbit. The X-15 withstood a taste of the searing heat that an orbital craft must face reentering the atmosphere. Some pilots ran into temperatures over 1300°F (704°C) when NASA scientists reckoned they would encounter only 800° to 1200°F (427° to 649°C).

From 1959 until 1968, the X-15 flew 199 times, providing information about *hypersonic flight* that would prove crucial to the creation and development of the space shuttle. As astronaut and first shuttle commander John Young remarked in *Shuttle,* "They were very similar programs and there was a great deal of feedback from the X-15 into the shuttle. It really paid off."

THE SHUTTLE BOOSTERS

The space shuttle, or Orbiter, has three basic functions in the course of a flight: it must launch like a rocket, orbit like a spacecraft, and land like an aircraft. All technical aspects of the shuttle are geared to achieve these three goals.

The space shuttle is powered by an unusual combination of engines and booster rockets: two solid rocket boosters (SRBs) and one massive external tank containing liquid hydrogen with liquid oxygen to burn it.

The shuttle is the first manned space vehicle to be even partly powered by solid rocket fuel. Rockets generally use fuels consisting of supercold liquid hydrogen, oxidized (or, more simply, burned) by liquid oxygen. Since hydrogen is the lightest element, it weighs far less than other rocket fuels, such as kerosene. The solid rocket boosters used for the shuttle contain two basic ingredients: atomized aluminum powder as a fuel and ammonium perchlorate as the oxidizer, the "burn" agent. When mixed together with iron oxide and treated with a plastic binder, the resulting solid rocket fuel is poured into the SRB casings where it reaches the consistency of hard rubber. The SRBs are then attached to the Orbiter's external tank.

In a shuttle launch, the twin SRBs fire up after the main engines begin, lifting the craft to an altitude of about 27 miles (43.5 km) in two minutes. After this altitude is achieved, the now empty SRBs are jettisoned with small clusters of rockets from the larger external tank. Because they are reusable, the boosters are parachuted into the ocean, where they are picked up by a recovery ship.

The tremendous external tank actually consists of two tanks: 141,000 gallons (5,300 hectoliters) of liquid oxygen in front and 385,000 gallons (14,600 hectoliters) of liquid hydrogen in the back. Unlike the SRBs, which are boosters unto themselves, the external tank pumps fuel through the

Orbiter's three main engines in the rear of the craft. There the liquid elements are converted to gases and the fiery mixture is squeezed through the conical engines. The added thrust of the external tank boosts the shuttle up to an altitude of 70 miles (113 km), near earth orbit. At this point, eight minutes into the mission, the external tank is jettisoned from the Orbiter. Most of the tank is designed to burn up in the outer reaches of the atmosphere; its charred fragments are intended to fall in little-navigated parts of the Indian Ocean.

Orbit is finally achieved about four minutes later with thrust from the two smaller rocket engines located on opposite sides of the Orbiter's main engines. These engines, known as the orbital maneuvering system, will fire twice to place the shuttle in a reliable orbit to continue with its mission.

To keep the shuttle in a stable orbit, a series of thrusters called the reaction control system (RCS) is employed. The RCS uses thirty-eight thrusters to control the shuttle's orbital direction. For even more exacting maneuvers, there are an additional six smaller thrusters. This total of forty-four thrusters, located at the rear and in the nose of the shuttle, makes it a highly spaceworthy craft.

The most dangerous part of an orbital mission is still reentry, and as studies with the X-15 had shown, winged spacecraft are far more susceptible to punishing heat than the simpler capsule designs. What was needed was a covering for the shuttle that would allow the pilots to fly through the fiery friction generated in the upper atmosphere.

To protect the Orbiter from heat, a material known as reinforced carbon-carbon is used for the nosecap and the most heat-prone edges of the Orbiter's small wings. For further protection, tile was developed that would cover the Orbiter's surface and insulate it from reentry heat intense enough to melt steel. Based on silicon, which is found in ordinary sand, these tiles can withstand temperatures of up to 3000°F (1650°C). Although some heat tiles have fallen off in early shuttle orbital flight tests, there has never been any danger to the crew from the rigors of reentry.

PREPARING THE SHUTTLE

With its fuel tanks attached, the space shuttle is far too large to be moved onto a launch pad. The problem was how to assemble the separate parts of the shuttle *on* the launchpad.

The assembly of the shuttle takes place in the Kennedy Space Center's Vehicle Assembly Building (VAB), a huge structure where the Apollo/Saturn V was assembled. The VAB covers 8 acres (3 hectares) and stands

525 feet (160 m) tall. Its single-interior space is so large that clouds have been known to form near the ceiling.

The launchpad, a structure so immense as to dwarf the shuttle itself, is right there inside the VAB too. The Orbiter sits on a mobile launchpad, one that rolls ever so slowly out of the VAB, up a steady 5-degree incline and out to the launching area. This Mobile Launch Platform (MLP), first used for the Apollo missions, is put in motion by the Crawler-Transporter.

Weighing 6 million pounds, or 2.7 million kg (11 million pounds, or 5 million kg, fully loaded with shuttle and launch platform), the Crawler is propelled by four giant tanklike treads. Taking into account the inestimably heavy—and expensive—load the Crawler carries, its maximum speed of about 1 mile (1.6 km) per hour is not unreasonable. At the end of the Crawler's slow-motion journey to the launching area, it slips out from under the Mobile Launch Platform and leaves it sitting on its "pedestals." From there the Crawler lumbers back to the Vehicle Assembly Building.

THE *ENTERPRISE*

The first space shuttle ever built was never launched. It was originally to be named the *Constitution*, but fans of the *Star Trek* television show flooded NASA with letters asking that America's first true spaceship be named the *Enterprise*. President Gerald Ford approved the renaming. The space shuttle *Enterprise* was officially unveiled in September 1976 with nearly the entire cast of *Star Trek* on hand. Although the first manned test flights of the shuttle were conducted with the *Enterprise*, it was never launched out of the atmosphere. Eventually, it was used for spare parts for the rest of the shuttle fleet.

When the space agency started wondering what to name this new fleet of shuttles, one NASA official suggested that they be named after old British fighting ships. President Jimmy Carter thought that it would make more sense to name them after *American* fighting (and exploration) ships. That is how the shuttles came to be called *Atlantis, Columbia, Challenger,* and *Enterprise* (the real *Enterprise* is one of the largest aircraft carriers ever built). The only exception is *Discovery,* which is named after two British exploration vessels that were in use before the United States declared its independence from Great Britain.

The first thing the new shuttle was tested for was its ability to safely return to earth from orbit. And just as the X-15 rode atop a Boeing B-52 for its test flights, so the shuttle *Enterprise* was tested from atop a Boeing 747. Specially modified to carry and release the shuttle, the NASA 747 would have to reach the same velocity and approach that the shuttle

The shuttle Enterprise *rides piggy-back aboard a NASA jet during a landing test.*

would after reentering the atmosphere. These early atmospheric tests were called the Approach and Landing Tests (ALT) conducted at the Dryden Flight Research Center near Edwards Air Force Base. Astronauts Joe Engle and Dick Truly were one *Enterprise* crew, alternating with Fred Haise and Gordon Fullerton. (Haise was the designated lunar module pilot in the unlucky but resourceful *Apollo 13* crew.) On the earliest ALT flights, the shuttle was never detached from the 747. Then, on August 12, 1977, the shuttle *Enterprise* broke free of the 747 and coasted smoothly to the Dryden runway. Haise and Fullerton proved that this new spaceship, despite its boxy appearance, could glide home like a bird.

ON BOARD THE SHUTTLE

Crews aboard the shuttle live on Houston time, getting up at about 6:00 A.M. to float down to the galley for breakfast. There is no need for space-suits once the shuttle is in orbit; the crew is allowed to wear comfortable earth clothes. Although shoes are only occasionally worn in orbit, when they are worn, they are suction shoes to keep the crew on the floor. The cabin temperature never goes above 90°F (32°C) nor below 61°F (16°C). Air inside the shuttle is fresh and free of pollen.

In the cockpit behind the Orbiter's front windows, the mission commander sits on the left side on the flight deck with his pilot on the right. To fly the shuttle, a dizzying assembly of controls, switches, and instrument panels are needed. They cover every square inch in the cockpit. Behind the commander and pilot's stations are seats for two other crew members. These are removed once the shuttle is in orbit.

The crew compartments, where the shuttle team eats, sleeps, and cooks, are located below the flight deck. One crew member cooks three daily meals for the others, and then another cooks the next day. Menus on the shuttle have progressed greatly since the squeeze-tube days of the Mercury and Gemini progams. Shuttle crews now choose between sliced beef with barbecue sauce and shrimp creole, or between broccoli au gratin and chicken à la king.

All orbiters are equipped with the best sanitation equipment in space. In a weightless environment, the simple act of washing your hands could turn into an attack of gallons of free-floating water droplets, which could easily short-circuit electronic systems on the spacecraft. To channel the water, a jet of air keeps it flowing in a steady stream in one direction. When the astronaut washes his or her hands, for example, the water is blown over the hands and out a drain to the waste-water storage tanks. The zero-gravity toilet works on this same air-flow principle.

The flight deck of the space shuttle Orbiter

Anna Fisher (right) demonstrates how astronauts aboard the shuttle use the treadmill to get exercise. David Walker (left) narrates for the TV audience.

Although space flight is exciting, shuttle crews have to sleep sometime. The shuttle has seats for ten, but there are only four sleep stations on board. Needless to say, there is shuttle activity going on around the clock, so crew members sleep at staggered hours. Because some must sleep while the rest work, nappers are supplied with eye masks, earplugs, and sound-suppression blankets. Restraint belts keep the sleeping astronaut from floating out of bed.

THE *CHALLENGER* DISASTER

As every American is aware, the greatest tragedy of the U.S. space program occurred on January 28, 1986, when the space shuttle *Challenger* burst into flames shortly after launch. On board the Orbiter were commander Francis Scobee, pilot Michael Smith, mission specialist Judith Resnik, mission specialist Ronald McNair, mission specialist Ellison Onizuka, payload specialist Gregory Jarvis, and payload specialist Christa McAuliffe—who had been well publicized as the first teacher in space. The *Challenger* disaster was a national tragedy that also posed the most significant challenge to NASA's competence as a space agency since the *Apollo 1* fire.

After three days of launch delays, the twenty-fifth space shuttle mission, 51-L, lifted off from the Kennedy Space Center on a mission to deploy two satellites, conduct scientific experiments, and to have Christa McAuliffe conduct lessons to be broadcast on public television. About seventy-four seconds into the flight and 15 miles (24km) downrange from the launchpad, the external tank exploded and the *Challenger* was enveloped in flames. All lives aboard were lost.

President Ronald Reagan appointed a commission to investigate the disaster, headed by former secretary of state William Rogers. Commission members included Sally Ride, the first American woman in space, and Chuck Yeager, the first man to break the sound barrier. After four months of investigation, the findings of the Rogers Commission were published.

The report cited faulty seals on the solid rocket boosters as the probable cause of the explosion. The morning of the liftoff was exceptionally cold for Florida, and this may have damaged the rubber O-ring gaskets that hold parts of the SRB casing together. In this weakened state, the gaskets broke, and escaping hot gases blew out of the SRB and onto the external fuel tank. At almost the same time, the damaged SRB broke loose from its support and struck the liquid hydrogen tank. The combination of escaping gases and the impact of the SRB caused the external tank to explode, dooming the *Challenger* crew.

The Challenger crew. Front row (left to right): Michael Smith, Dick Scobee, Ronald McNair. Back row (left to right): Ellison Onizuka, Christa McAuliffe, Gregory Jarvis, Judith Resnick.

The ocean floor near Cape Canaveral was searched
for remains of the Challenger. Wreckage was examined
for clues to the cause of the explosion.

In the Rogers Commission Report, blame fell equally on the subcontractor, Morton-Thiokol, for manufacturing a faulty booster, and on NASA for not catching the problem while there was time. Both were cited for ignoring warnings that questioned the reliability of the O-rings. There were some engineers who saw the dangers of the SRB rocket joint, but no one paid them the attention they deserved.

The *Challenger* disaster may have been NASA's greatest setback, but the Space Transportation System flights will continue, after a period of careful self-examination. The mistakes that led up to the shuttle explosion have made some hard truths apparent: that the dangers of space flight must never be underestimated, and that the need to proceed into space is even more compelling now than it ever was before.

11

JOHN W. YOUNG
First to Command
the Space Shuttle

When John Young took charge of the previously unflown Orbiter *Columbia* and drove it dramatically into the cosmos, it was the first time that many people had ever heard of him. Yet John Young has been an active force in the U.S. space program since he squeezed himself into the first Gemini capsule alongside Gus Grissom. Young is a Gemini veteran, an Apollo moonwalker, and the first person to fly the space shuttle. Actually, John Young has another "first" to his credit. He's the first American to travel in space *six* times, and he's still flying. John Young is simply America's top astronaut, bar none.

NAVY FIGHTER PILOT

John Watts Young was born on September 24, 1930, in San Francisco. He grew up in Florida, where he graduated from Orlando High School. John enrolled immediately at the Georgia Institute of Technology, where he would receive a bachelor of science degree in aeronautical engineering with highest honors in 1952. (When John Young was still a student at the Georgia Institute of Technology, he went to Florida to survey grounds for possible rocket launch sites. In the years to come, that area he had inspected would become the launching area for all manned U.S. space projects, Cape Canaveral.)

When Young left Georgia Tech, he enlisted in the U.S. Navy. He spent one year on board the destroyer U.S.S. *Laws* before being sent to train with helicopters, jets, and propeller-driven aircraft. After this training, John Young was assigned to Fighter Squadron 103 where he flew Cougars and Crusaders for four years. During this time, John Young was married to the former Susy Feldman, and the two later raised daughter Sandy and son John.

In 1959, Young attended United States Navy Test Pilot School and then worked at the Naval Air Test Center for the next three years, where he flew Crusader and Phantom fighter-jets. Then in 1962, John Young would find his true calling: he was chosen for NASA's Astronaut Group 2.

GEMINI

On *Gemini 3*, John Young was the very first Group 2 astronaut to fly in space accompanied by "veteran" Gus Grissom. *Gemini 3* was only a three-orbit flight, but it proved that the orbit of a spacecraft could be changed to another, whether higher or lower. Still, the Gemini capsule was as yet untested, and the *Gemini 3* crew wondered about a thousand things that could go wrong. When they worried about the status of their stabilizing thrusters, John Young made a bit of irreverent space history.

Young told *Spaceflight*:

Well, we were over the middle of the Pacific Ocean on a night orbital pass. The sensors that we were using to align the platform weren't working right, so we weren't getting a good platform alignment. First Gus was somewhat nervous about that because we knew if we didn't have the platform aligned properly when we fired the retro-rockets, we might be pointed in the wrong direction, which would leave you up there for a long time. So we were very nervous about that, and as we came over that part of the ocean I knew that until we got into daylight and could see which way we're supposed to be aligned, it was really no sense worrying about it. So I handed Gus a corned beef sandwich and said, "Here, try this while you're thinking about how to get this platform aligned." And he said I'd get in a lot of trouble over it because there was no mustard on it. He was right about that.

After the flight, the remnants of the sandwich were encased in plastic and put on display on Young's desk (alongside an official reprimand from the less-than-amused NASA directors).

John Young's second space flight, *Gemini 10*, flew in a higher orbit than had ever been reached by a spacecraft before—467 miles (752 km) up. Young took the opportunity to radio back his pithy comment, "Columbus was right; the world *is* round."

Crewed by Young and Mike Collins, the mission of *Gemini 10* was to demonstrate that a spacecraft could dock with another vehicle in space, then boost itself into a higher orbit and dock *a second time* with another target vehicle.

During one docking with an Agena, Mike Collins walked in space—actually "swam" in space—over to the orbiting rocket. Then Collins also did something that travelers the world over do every year, only he did it in space. He was the first person to lose a camera during a space flight. It simply drifted out of his hands and eventually into the atmosphere.

There were a couple of problems meeting the Agena. As Young remarked to *Spaceflight*, "We came right into the sunlight, I guess, and overshot the vehicle and then had to use a lot of propellant to get there, but we got there."

The *Gemini 10* mission was a total success, not counting Mike Collins's lost snapshots. They splashed down in the Atlantic, where they were picked up by the U.S.S. *Guadalcanal*.

APOLLO

When John Young orbited the moon in the command module during the *Apollo 10* mission, he was paving the way for the moon travelers who would follow him. He may not have known that one of those moon travelers would be John Young as commander of *Apollo 16*.

The *Apollo 10* flight was a dry run for the lunar *Apollo 11* mission. You had to empathize with astronauts Tom Stafford and Gene Cernan, dropping the lunar module down close to the moon's surface but not able to land there. During the *Apollo 10* flight, Young kept the command module *Charlie Brown* in lunar orbit while Tom Stafford and Gene Cernan descended to within 9 miles (14.5 km) of the moon's surface in the lunar module *Snoopy*. (John Young described the LM *Snoopy* in lunar orbit to *Life*: "When he was way out there, 100 miles [160 km] or more, he looked like an ordinary star in the daytime and a flashing star at night."

During the ascent stage of the flight of the *Snoopy*, when the ascent rocket was supposed to send them into docking position with the command module, the LM went into a spin not unlike that of the *Gemini 8* crisis. After some tense moments, the LM docked successfully with the command module.

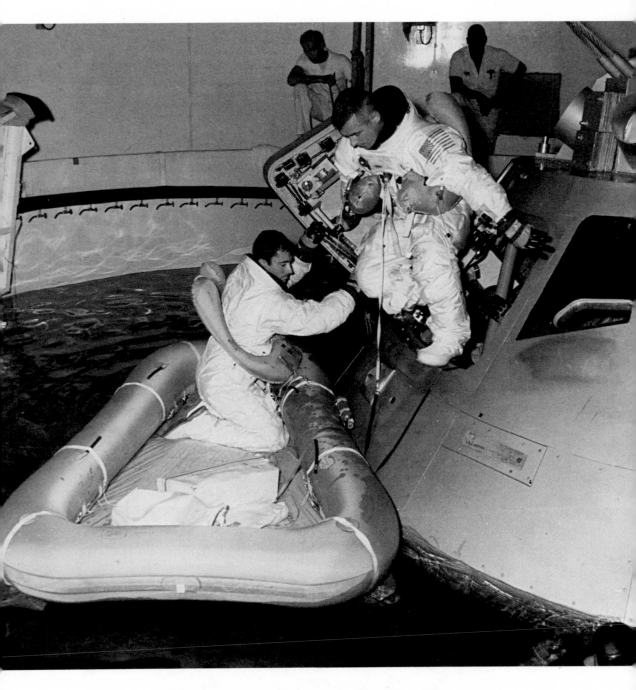

John Young (in life raft) and Eugene Cernan practice water egress, part of the Apollo training program.

"Tom and Gene coasted out 150 miles [240 km] in front of *Charlie Brown*," Young told *Life*, "down to less than 9 miles [14.5 km] from the lunar surface, and up again over the top of *Charlie Brown* and me by 120 miles [190 km], and behind us 350 miles [560 km]. One of our happiest moments was when we had rendezvoused and docked. . . . It was pretty good to see Tom's and Gene's faces as they crawled back through the tunnel." *Apollo 10* returned safely home to a Pacific splashdown and the U.S.S. *Princeton*.

Apollo 16 roared off the launchpad under the searing power of a Saturn V rocket that would provide it with enough thrust to reach the moon's Descartes region. John Young and Charles Duke would perform the lunar EVA and Tom Mattingly would orbit the moon waiting for their return.

When Young set foot out of the LM and onto the lunar surface, he said: "Here you are, mysterious and unknown Descartes highland plains. *Apollo 16* is going to change your image."

Like many astronauts, John Young loves fast cars. During *Apollo 16*, when Young was driving across the moonscape in the Lunar Rover, he'd "floor it" to top speeds and then make sharp turns to test the grip of the tires. As a result, John Young may be considered the first hot-rodder in outer space. Unfortunately, there was nobody there for him to race.

After *Apollo 16* there was only one other area of space flight that John Young hadn't tackled: the space shuttle.

SHUTTLE

From only a brief account of his life, one can understand why John Young was chosen to command the shuttle on its maiden flight. The two-man crew of Young and Robert Crippen were old pros, but even John Young was a bit nervous. "NASA doesn't pay you to express anxieties and fears," he told *National Geographic*, "I was probably less confident of total success than most of our people."

Doubts or no doubts, the shuttle's main and solid tanks ignited just right at 7:00 A.M. on the morning of April 12, 1981. To attest to the space-worthiness of the shuttle *Columbia*, live television pictures from the shuttle were broadcast less than two hours after launch.

Young and Crippen found their new orbiting home to be perfect. "Because of zero g, it was more fun to zoom down below into the mid-deck to do a checkout," Young told *National Geographic*. "Bob Crippen thought so too. He was learning to swim in space pretty quickly."

The flight of STS-1, the first orbital space shuttle mission, lasted for thirty-six orbits. John Young and Bob Crippen gave the new spacecraft

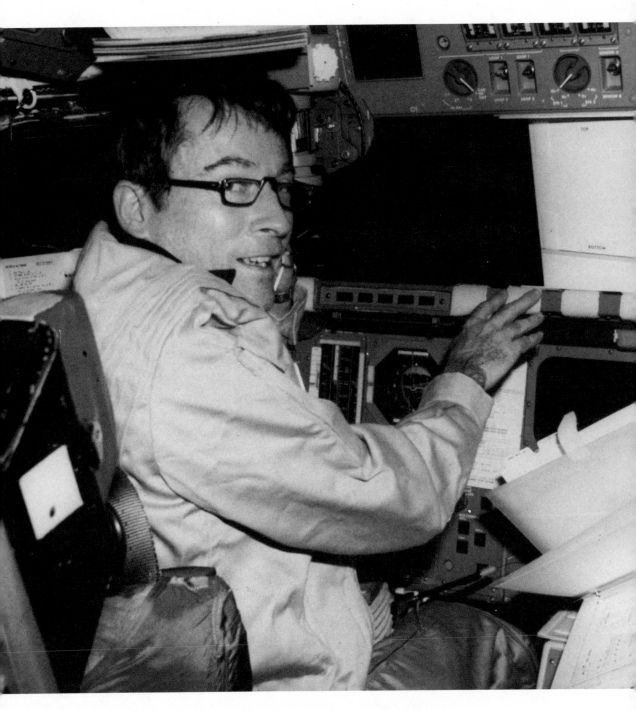

*John Young at the commander's
station of the* Columbia

high marks. As Young told *National Geographic,* "The Orbiter is a joy to fly. It does what you tell it to, even in very unstable regions."

When the space shuttle makes its return to earth, it must literally turn around until it faces backward in orbit and then it fires its tail-end rockets. This slows the Orbiter down for reentry. Ultimately, the shuttle approaches the runway at about 200 miles (320 km) per hour. For the blistering heat of reentry, the shuttle is covered over with heat-resistant tiles that can withstand temperatures of up to 3000°F (1650°C).

THE CHIEF ASTRONAUT

John Young's sixth flight was the mission of STS-9, which was the first to bring the European Spacelab into orbit. Since the weighty Spacelab was returning home with the *Columbia,* it made the Orbiter the *heaviest* shuttle ever to try to land at Edwards Air Force Base. Under John Young's steady hand, the shuttle landed smoothly.

Since 1975 John Young has been the Chief of the Astronaut Office, a position of great authority within NASA. But no matter what his earthly successes may be, John Young always keeps an eye to the skies.

Bob Crippen quoted John Young as saying after the shuttle *Columbia* touched ground: "We're really not that far, the human race isn't, from going to the stars."

12

SALLY K. RIDE
First American Woman
in Space

The flight of Sally Kristen Ride was thought to be a milestone for the American space program and American women alike. Everyone was impressed by her achievement, except for Sally Ride. As Sally remarked to *Time*, "It's too bad that society isn't to the point yet where the country could just send up a woman astronaut and nobody would think twice about it." Indeed, there should be nothing at all remarkable about a woman in space, but that doesn't mean that Sally Ride is anything less than remarkable herself.

FROM TENNIS COURTS
TO ADVANCED PHYSICS

Sally Ride was born in Los Angeles, California, on May 26, 1951, the daughter of Dr. and Mrs. Dale B. Ride. Dr. Ride is a professor of political science. Sally and her sister, Karen, grew up in the suburban town of Encino, California, where Sally developed an early interest in science and athletics. From her primary schooling through to her winning a partial scholarship at Los Angeles's private Westlake High School, Sally was a straight-A student. Sally told *Time* that her parents seldom pressured her about what she wanted to do, "except to make sure I studied and brought home the right kind of grades." As Sally's interest in science grew, so did her success at tennis.

Sally Ride started college at Swarthmore, in Pennsylvania, but later transferred to Stanford University, back in California, where she graduated with both a bachelor of science degree in physics and a bachelor of arts degree in English. An odd combination of interests, but Sally Ride saw Shakespeare and Einstein as equally fascinating. Where most people would choose between the two disciplines, she simply studied both. "My parents must have done a great job," she told *People* magazine, "Anytime I wanted to pursue something that they weren't familiar with, that was not part of their lifestyle, they let me go ahead and do it."

The other serious interest in her life, tennis, was becoming less and less important to her. Although Sally was a nationally ranked junior who had received encouragement from tennis great Billie Jean King, she returned to Stanford to do advanced graduate work in physics. After performing research in experimental general relativity, X-ray astrophysics, and free-electron laser physics, Sally Ride graduated from Stanford with a Ph.D. in Physics.

A NEW GROUP OF ASTRONAUTS

Shortly before she received her doctorate, Sally Ride saw a notice in the campus newspaper that NASA was looking for astronaut-scientists. She sent in a postcard. Out of 8,370 applicants, she was one of the thirty-five chosen by NASA as Astronaut Group 8. This was the first time women had been accepted into the astronaut corps. "From the astronaut-office point of view, it wasn't a man's world when I was accepted along with five other women in 1978," Sally explained in *Vogue*. "The attitude of both men and women in the astronaut program was not, were you a man or a woman, but could you do the job?" As Sally Ride and other women astronauts such as Anna Fisher, Shannon Lucid, Judith Resnik, Rhea Seddon, and Kathryn Sullivan would prove, women could *certainly* do the job.

The combination of men and women astronauts has had some unexpected results: astronauts getting married. Sally Ride was one of the three married astronaut couples currently in the space program. She and her husband are in the process of being divorced. Sally met her husband, Dr. Steven A. Hawley, in astronaut training, and on July 24, 1982, they were married at his parents' home in Salina, Kansas. She flew herself in a small aircraft to her informal wedding (she wore levis and a rugby shirt), which was presided over by the groom's father and the bride's sister—both Presbyterian ministers! (Like Sally Ride and Steven Hawley, married astronauts Robert Gibson and Rhea Seddon also met in training, but Drs. Bill and Anna Fischer were already married before entering the astronaut corps.)

Sally Ride was officially designated a mission specialist—a different sort of astronaut from the test pilots of the early programs. A mission specialist must have a college degree in science or engineering, and advanced degrees are preferable. A mission specialist must work for at least three years in his or her area of specialty—for Sally Ride, it was in X-ray astrophysics. As she told *People* of the new astronaut trainees, "We're really all very similar. We're all people who are dedicated to the space program and who really want to fly in the space shuttle. That's a common characteristic that we all have that transcends the different backgrounds."

The mission specialists are full-time astronauts. They must know almost everything about the operations of the shuttle, aside from their individual areas of expertise. When someone is chosen as a mission specialist, the first thing he or she does is take courses in the basic sciences, as well as guidance and navigation, meteorology, astronomy, computers, physics, and mathematics. A great deal of time is spent flying, even though mission specialists aren't required to know how to fly an aircraft.

Aside from shuttle pilots and mission specialists, another group travels into space on the shuttle: the payload specialists. A payload specialist is *not* a full-time astronaut. The payload specialists are in orbit to operate or launch a specific device. They are trained principally by the sponsors of the payloads they accompany into space, but they also receive 150 hours of NASA training. This training explains something about the shuttle and its "housekeeping" chores, as well as emergency procedures.

A RIDE IN THE SHUTTLE

"I did not come to NASA to make history," Sally Ride told *Newsweek*. "It's important to me that people don't think I was picked for the flight because I am a woman and it's time for NASA to send one." On June 18, 1983, when Sally Ride went into orbit aboard shuttle *Challenger* flight STS-7, she went with the full confidence of her crewmates, who included Rick Hauck, John Fabian, and Norman Thagard.

Shuttle commander Robert Crippen, who made the first orbital flight with John Young, had the utmost faith in the abilities of Sally Ride. "She is flying with us because she is the very best person for the job," he told *MacLean's*. "There is no man I would rather have in her place." He continued to praise her in *Time*: "You like people who stay calm under duress. And Sally can do that. She hit all the squares."

Sally reacts amusingly at seasoned astronaut Robert Crippen's new-found feminism. "Crip won't even open a door for me anymore," she told *Time*.

Despite the preparedness she gained from using flight simulators, nothing could prepare her for the thrill of the shuttle lifting off, catapulted skyward by its powerful boosters. "The engines light, the solids light, and all of a sudden you know you're *going*," she recalled in *Vogue*. "It's over-whelming. There is nothing like it."

The major job that Sally Ride prepared for was the manipulation of the remote manipulator system (RMS), a 50-foot (15-m) -long mechanical arm that protrudes from the left side of the Orbiter's cargo bay and is operated from the rear of the shuttle flight deck. The RMS was developed by the Canadian government and is sometimes called the Canadarm. Like a human arm, the remote manipulator system has a "shoulder," "elbow," and "wrist," with a mechanical "hand" at the end. Each robotic joint is powered by six small motors. The arm is also equipped with TV cameras to allow operators to get a closer look at their work.

The Canadarm enables mission specialists inside the Orbiter to pick up and place satellites in orbit from the cargo bay, as well as to pull satellites out of orbit and place them into the bay. "I spent two years on it, and nothing else," she remarked in *Newsweek*. "As far as I knew, there was nothing else; what you did was launch an arm."

The RMS was used throughout the STS-7 flight, the second time the *Challenger* had flown in space. The German scientific package called the Shuttle Pallet Satellite, or SPAS, was deployed and retrieved by the Can-adarm. The SPAS helped astronauts understand what happens to satellites when placed into orbit from the shuttle. It also proved to be good practice with the Canadarm. The *Challenger* and the SPAS conducted the first formation flying of an Orbiter and a free-flying satellite. Flushed with the success of the remote manipulator system, commander Bob Crippen radioed to Houston, "We've been told that some crews in the past have announced, 'We deliver.' Well, for flight seven, we pick up and deliver."

Sally Ride was equally ebullient about the success of shuttle flight STS-7. "The thing that I'll remember most about the flight is that it was fun,"

Mission specialist Sally Ride communicates with ground control from the deck of the Challenger.

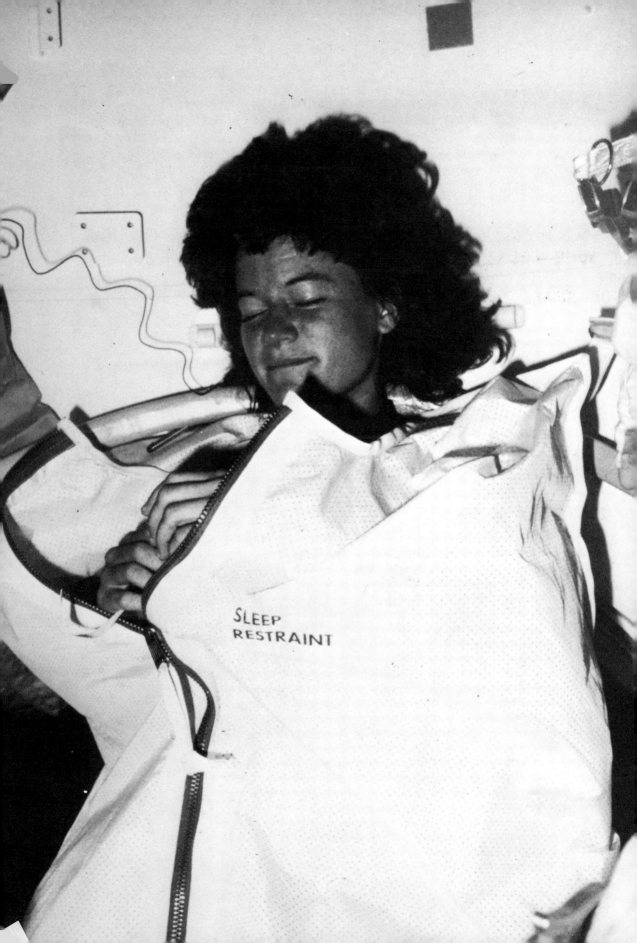

she told *Newsweek*. "In fact, I'm sure it was the most fun that I will ever have in my life."

A CAREER IN SPACE

Before she ever flew in the shuttle, Sally Ride told *People*, "My intention after the flight is to come back to the astronaut office and get back in line and try and fly again. I'd like to do it as many times as NASA will let me." And that is exactly what she did. Her next flight was STS-41-G, launched on October 5, 1984, and commanded again by Robert Crippen. The shuttle was piloted by Jon McBride, with mission specialists (besides Sally Ride) Dr. Kathryn Sullivan and David Leetsma and payload specialists Paul Scully-Power and Canadian Marc Garneau aboard. The crew conducted extensive mapping from the bird's-eye view of earth orbit. Kathryn Sullivan became the first American woman to walk in space. The *Challenger* touched ground at the Kennedy Space Center at Cape Canaveral on October 13, 1984.

Reluctantly, Sally Ride has become an authentic American space hero. As she commented in *Vogue*, "I didn't particularly care that I was the role model, but I thought it was important that somebody be."

Even the nation's great repository of historical artifacts, the Smithsonian Institution, asked for the flight suit that Sally Ride wore into space. Donating the suit to the Smithsonian, she quipped to *Vogue*, "This was the closest thing to me during the flight."

After the *Challenger* disaster in January 1986, Sally Ride served on the Presidential Commission on the Space Shuttle *Challenger* Accident, or the Rogers Commission. She was roundly applauded for the hard work and long hours she put in for the Commission. In August 1986, Sally Ride was assigned a post at NASA headquarters in Washington as the special assistant to the administrator for strategic planning. In her career as in space, Sally Ride is a hard woman to keep tied down. During the fall of 1987 she assumed the position of Science Fellow at the Stanford University Center for International Security and Arms Control in Palo Alto, California.

A candid photo of Sally Ride napping. The sleep restraint serves as a bed in weightlessness.

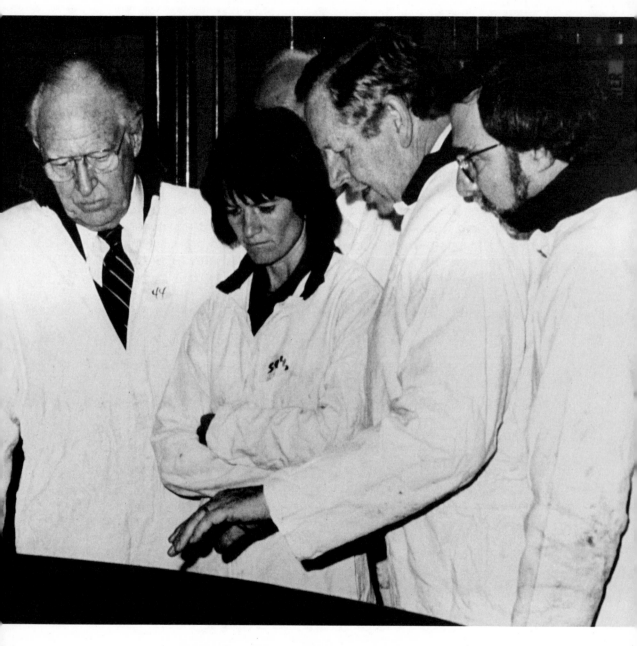

The chair of the commission investigating
the Challenger *disaster, William Rogers (left),*
and commission member Sally Ride talk to
officials at Kennedy Space Center.

When she left the astronaut corps, NASA administrator James C. Fletcher praised Sally Ride's contributions to the American space effort, saying, "Her flight as the first American woman in space firmly established an equal role for women in the space exploration program. Today, the assignment of women to Shuttle crews is a routine matter based on ability and need and is no longer a cause for notice."

13

GUION S. BLUFORD, JR.
First Black American
in Space

Guion Bluford will be remembered in American history as a black man who crossed a previously insurmountable color barrier, as baseball's Jackie Robinson had done years earlier. Yet Guy Bluford, now famous as the first black American in space, prefers to think of himself as a highly trained aerospace engineer, astronaut, and, as he described himself in *Newsweek*, "a warm, quietish person who loves airplanes." Without any flash or fanfare, Bluford has proven himself to be an astronaut of unassailable stature—and a man of action as well as learning. "I don't view what I do as heroic," he told *Ebony*, "but maybe that's because I have a strong understanding of aviation, aerodynamics, spacecraft, and flying."

FROM PHILADELPHIA
TO CAM RANH BAY

Guion S. Bluford, Jr., was born in West Philadelphia, Pennsylvania, on November 22, 1942. Guion lived with his parents, Guion, Sr., and Lolita, and his brothers, Kenneth and Eugene, in an integrated row-house neighborhood on Media Street. Called "Bunny" by his family, Guion was shy and preferred working out puzzles or brain-teasers to playing outside. He was a prolific builder of model airplanes, but unlike other boys his age, he was more interested in the aerodynamics of flight than in actually flying an

*Guion Bluford at a press conference
before his space shuttle flight*

airplane. By junior high, with his interest in the sciences blossoming, Guion Bluford decided to be an aerospace engineer.

Fortunately for Guy Bluford, he didn't take the advice of a high school counselor who thought he wouldn't do well in college. In 1960, Bluford enrolled at Penn State University, where he studied hard and joined the campus Air Force ROTC program. He graduated with a bachelor of science degree in aerospace engineering. At about this time, Bluford married Linda Tull, from his hometown of Philadelphia. Guion and Linda had two sons, Guion Stewart Bluford, III, and James Trevor Bluford.

Following his ROTC preparation, Guy Bluford joined the Air Force to fly in Vietnam. He was trained in Arizona at Williams Air Force Base and received his pilot's wings in January 1965. In 1967 he was in the 557th Tactical Fighter Squadron, flying F-4C jet aircraft out of Cam Ranh Bay. During his time in Vietnam, Bluford flew 144 combat missions, sixty-five of which were over risky North Vietnamese targets. For his service in Vietnam, Guion Bluford received the National Defense Service Medal, the Vietnam Campaign Medal, the Vietnam Cross of Gallantry with Palm, the Vietnam Service Medal, and ten Air Force Air Medals.

After his combat service, the much-decorated Guion Bluford returned to the United States, where he became an instructor pilot for T-38A aircraft, an evaluation officer, and an assistant flight commander at Sheppard Air Force Base in Texas.

In the summer of 1972, Bluford entered the Air Force Institute of Technology at Wright-Patterson Air Force Base in Ohio. After he had earned his master of science degree in aerospace engineering, Bluford was assigned to the Air Force Flight Dynamics Laboratory at Wright-Patterson. In 1978, he received a Ph.D in aerospace engineering, with a minor in laser physics. In January of that same year, Guion Bluford was accepted by NASA as a Group 8 astronaut.

CHALLENGER MISSION STS-8

The first black astronauts in the space program were Guion Bluford, Ronald McNair, and Frederick Gregory—all members of Group 8. In Group 9, another black astronaut joined, Charles Bolden. In the early days of the

At the Johnson Space Center, Bluford demonstrates a treadmill experiment to be conducted on the space shuttle.

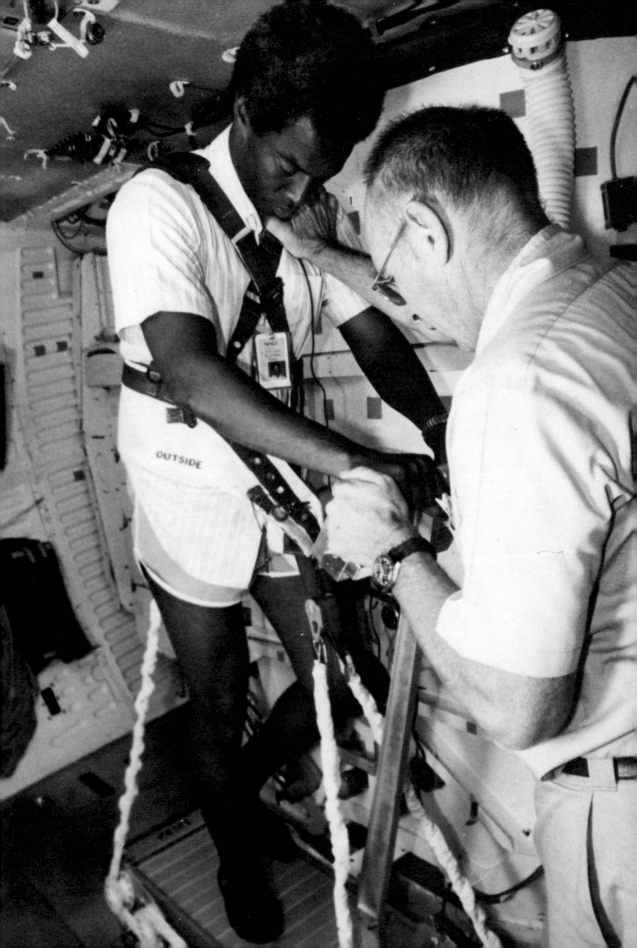

manned space program, astronauts were required to be "test pilots, and that's a very small, elite group of people that includes very few blacks," Guion Bluford told *Ebony*. Still, Bluford joined NASA because it was relevant to his personal areas of study. He told *Newsweek*, "The Space Program was an expansion of what I was already doing. . . . " Before his first space flight, he worked with the remote manipulator system, Spacelab 3 experiments, shuttle systems, the Shuttle Avionics Integration Laboratory, and the Flight Systems laboratory.

Although he would rather dedicate himself to his aerospace research than civil rights breakthroughs, Guy Bluford is aware that he is "setting the pace, setting the example of those behind me," as he remarked to *Newsweek*.

For STS-8, the space shuttle *Challenger* was launched at night—the first night launch in shuttle history. At 2:32 A.M. on August 30, 1983, the Orbiter headed spaceward with its crew of Guion Bluford, commander Richard Truly, pilot Daniel Brandenstein, and mission specialists Dale Gardner and Dr. William E. Thornton.

One of the primary objectives of mission STS-8 was the deployment of INSAT-1B, the Indian National Satellite. This $45-million satellite would provide communications and weather information to India. During their second day in orbit, Guy Bluford deployed the INSAT perfectly.

Guion Bluford also took part in experiments of the continuous flow electrophoresis system—the electrical separation of biological fluids in space. It's hoped that the kind of research conducted by Bluford on STS-8 will lead to advances in important medicines that must be manufactured in space. During the same mission, a study was made of the biophysiological effects of space flight, to help NASA doctors further understand what is a largely unexplored, brand-new human condition—weightlessness.

The shuttle *Challenger*, which took off in the first night launch of the shuttle program, returned to earth with the first night landing of an Orbiter. The shuttle came to a halt at Edwards Air Force Base on September 5, 1983—ninety-eight orbits and 145 hours after liftoff. The mission of STS-8 was an unqualified success, and in the eyes of the nation, so was Guion Bluford.

ANOTHER STEP FORWARD

After Guion Bluford returned to earth, he embarked upon a wide-ranging speaking tour, a black astronaut sharing his experiences with Americans of all races. Who could guess that the kid they said wouldn't be able to keep up at college would end up receiving honorary Ph.D's from universities such as Florida A&M, Texas Southern, Virginia State, Morgan State,

Stevens Institute of Technology, Tuskegee Institute, Bowie State College, and Thomas Jefferson University!

"My flight on the shuttle was important because it represented another step forward," Guy Bluford told *Ebony*. "That flight will open the door for other blacks who want to get into the astronaut program, and it also indicates that opportunities do exist for black youngsters if they work hard and strive to take advantage of those opportunities."

14

BRUCE MCCANDLESS, II
First to Walk
Untethered in Space

When Bruce McCandless propelled himself across the sky with no tether or umbilical cord to restrain him, he fulfilled a dream of utter physical freedom. Rising out of the massive shuttle cargo bay, Bruce McCandless was the embodiment of unrestricted movement, caught neither in the grip of gravity nor within the airtight walls of the shuttle. After the mission of Bruce McCandless, people's ancient dream of flying like a bird would become exhilaratingly real.

NAVAL AIRCRAFT ACE

Although born in Boston on June 8, 1937, Bruce McCandless's schooling took place in Long Beach, California. Bruce graduated from Long Beach Senior High School and went on to the United States Naval Academy at Annapolis. He graduated with a bachelor of science degree in 1958, ranked second in a class of 899. After Annapolis, Bruce McCandless married the former Bernice Doyle. In the early 1960s they had two children, Bruce, III, and Tracy.

Immediately after his Naval Academy schooling, Bruce McCandless received training from the Naval Aviation Training Command at bases in Pensacola, Florida, and Kingsville, Texas. In March 1960, he was designated a naval aviator and quickly left for Key West, Florida. There McCandless was trained for carrier landing and weapons systems. From

1960 to 1964, he was assigned to Fighter Squadron 102 aboard the aircraft carriers U.S.S. *Forrestal* and *Enterprise*. Bruce McCandless served aboard the *Enterprise* while the United States was blockading any ship from sailing to Cuba—a dramatic gesture by President John Kennedy.

During his years in naval aviation, Bruce McCandless became proficient at flying such diverse aircraft as the T-33B Shootingstar, the T-38A Talon, the F-4B Phantom II, the F-6A Skyray, the F-11 Tiger, the TF-9J Cougar, the T-1 Seastar, the T-34B Mentor, and the Bell 47G helicopter.

Bruce McCandless earned his master of science degree in electrical engineering from Stanford University in 1965. Shortly thereafter, he joined the United States astronaut corps.

THE PATIENT ASTRONAUT

Bruce McCandless was a member of astronaut Group 5, which was officially formed in April 1966, in the latter days of the Gemini project. It would be eighteen years—in 1984—before Bruce McCandless would fly in space.

McCandless worked as CapCom during Neil Armstrong's moonwalk and as one of the astronaut support crew for the lunar mission *Apollo 14*. At the moment that *Apollo 14* commander Alan Shepard set foot on the moon, McCandless kiddingly told him, "Not bad for an old man."[1] Bruce McCandless was also the backup pilot for *Skylab 2*, and had to be intimately familiar with that complex space project.

Years were spent in the development of the device that McCandless would ride into fame—the manned maneuvering unit, or MMU. Built by the Martin Marietta Corporation, the MMU would provide an astronaut with an easily controllable jet pack that makes possible free, untethered extravehicular activity.

Bruce McCandless had a hand in the design of the $15-million MMU, which has been described as an armchair with no seat. Contained in the "arm rests" of the MMU are controls for twenty-four jets that puff out nitrogen gas. With each burst of gas, the MMU propels an astronaut through space under his or her own power.

FLASH GORDON AND BUCK ROGERS

It was the end of an eighteen-year wait when, on February 3, 1984, the shuttle *Challenger* sent Bruce McCandless into orbit along with commander Vance Brand, pilot Robert Gibson, and mission specialists Ronald

McNair and Robert Stewart. At the outset, shuttle mission 41-B was trouble-plagued.

The biggest problem to beset the crew was the loss of two highly sophisticated communications satellites with an estimated value of $150 million. A balloon used in a navigational experiment unexpectedly exploded, hurting no one but causing some major disappointments. Minor disappointments were everywhere as well: the flight-tested Canadarm became strangely stiff and unusable, and even the toilet backed up!

If 41-B was a mission starved for good news, that news was delivered by MMU. First Bruce McCandless and, later, Robert Stewart conducted the untethered EVA. Commander Vance Brand said, "They call each other Flash Gordon and Buck Rogers" (after the science-fiction heroes of the cartoons and movie serials of the thirties and forties).

When Bruce McCandless floated free of the *Challenger*, he exclaimed, "Hey, this is neat! That may have been one small step for Neil, but it's a heck of a big leap for me." As Bruce McCandless grew more used to the free maneuvering made possible by the MMU, the more pleased he became. "We sure have a nice flying machine. It feels real good out here, not at all like the freeway," he told his crewmates. Only one area needed improvement, however. When the unit was set on attitude-hold mode and the user tried to move forward without rotation, there were some problems. McCandless told the watching crew, "When you put in for a long translation, the thing shudders and rattles and shakes." However, problems couldn't be too grave, because Vance Brand allowed Bruce McCandless to "fly" away from the Orbiter twice, at distances of 150 and 320 feet (46 and 98 m). With the reliable MMU, he flew back as well. This type of EVA will be used to wrestle lost satellites back into the cargo bay, where they will be repaired, sent back into orbit, or brought back to earth.

Looking down from his EVA, McCandless saw Cape Canaveral on earth below. He said, "Oh, I got to see if I can get a picture of this."

Like Ed White and the other spacewalking astronauts, Bruce McCandless saw the universe all around him from outside the earth's atmosphere. He told his fellow astronauts, "The view you get out here is like the difference between a view you get flying a heavy aircraft and looking out

"Hey, this is neat!" said Bruce McCandless as he moves outside the shuttle without a tether or umbilical line.

little windows and compared to flying a helicopter at Mach 25. It really is a beautiful panorama."[2]

Maneuvering the MMU around to the front of the Shuttle, Bruce McCandless asked the crew, "Hey, you going to want the windows washed or anything while I'm out here?" When McCandless was finished with his EVA, he handed the manned maneuvering unit to Robert Stewart, saying, "Enjoy it. Have a ball."

After their history-making EVA, President Ronald Reagan called the astronauts from his California ranch and told them they had opened up "a new era for the world in space. You've shown both our commercial partners and our foreign partners . . . that man *does* have the tools to work effectively in space."

The crew of *Challenger* mission 41-B took their rousing successes and limited failures and brought them all back to earth with a new shuttle first. Theirs was the first Orbiter to land on the Kennedy Space Center runway, an especially convenient site for the rapidly reusable space shuttles. Previously, the Orbiters had to be mounted on a 747 in California and piggybacked all the way to Cape Canaveral.

The greatest achievement of flight 41-B was that of Bruce McCandless and the seatless armchair that made science fiction a reality. In the future, his exceptional flight will surely become commonplace.

15

THE FUTURE IN SPACE

If a book full of famous astronauts and their first achievements makes you think that all the frontiers of space have been explored, then you couldn't be more wrong. New astronauts join the space program all the time. In fact, fifteen astronaut candidates were chosen from almost 2,000 applicants in the summer of 1987. Among the newest astronauts is a general practitioner—a family doctor—named Mae C. Jemison (who's also the first black woman to enter the astronaut corps).

Plans have been in the works for years that chart our course through the solar system far beyond the year 2000. If anything, there will be more exploration and adventure in the next thirty years.

In the twenty-first century, the space around the earth, the moon, and the area in between will become to the future what the Mediterranean Sea was in ancient times. More and more satellites, probes, and manned spacecraft will crowd the orbital paths around the earth and the moon.

Travel to earth orbit will become increasingly commonplace as industry begins to reap the technological harvest of space. The moon provides the nearest natural resources in our solar system. With a fraction of earth's gravity and none of its atmosphere, the moon will be a very easy place from which to mine raw materials. Perhaps remote robotic units would land there in advance to clear the way for the people who would inevitably follow.

Three spaceports are proposed: one in earth orbit, one in lunar orbit, and one at Libration Point, the area between the earth and the moon where the pull of their respective gravities is equal. The Libration Point spaceport would become a center of transfer for people and cargo headed to and from the moon. A system of circulating transports would ferry space-dwellers from one installation to another. In the next century, *space* may well be the new crossroads of the world.

But there's so much more in the works. . . .

- Mass drivers and ion propulsion that can propel a spacecraft across the solar system
- Fully self-sustaining biospheres to support life even in deep space
- An experimental aerospace plane far more advanced than the space shuttle

And the Martian expeditions aren't that far off, either.

Talented young men and women will be needed for the manned exploration of Mars and its moons Phobos and Deimos.

Would *you* like to go?

Maybe the greatest events in space history haven't even happened yet.

In the future, people may live and work on space colonies orbiting the earth. This artist's concept shows a solar-powered space station and, to the left, its twin neighbor.

SOURCE NOTES

Chapter 2
1. Timothy B. Benford and Brian Wilkes, *The Space Program Quiz and Fact Book* (New York: Harper & Row, 1985).
2. *Life* (May 19, 1961).
3. *Space World* (April 1971).
4. Richard P. Hallion and Tom D. Crouch, eds., *Apollo: Ten Years Since Tranquillity Base* (Washington: Smithsonian Institution Press, 1979).

Chapter 3
1. Benford, *The Space Program Quiz and Fact Book.*
2. "Results of the First Manned Orbital Space Flight" (U.S. Government Printing Office, February 20, 1962).
3. Benford, *The Space Program Quiz and Fact Book.*
4. John Noble Wilford, *We Reach the Moon* (New York: New York Times, 1979).

Chapter 4
1. Wilford, *We Reach the Moon.*
2. Tony Osman, *Space History* (New York: St. Martin's Press, 1983).

Chapter 6
1. Benford, *The Space Program Quiz and Fact Book.*

Chapter 7
1. Osman, *Space History.*

Chapter 8
1. Wilford, *We Reach the Moon.*

Chapter 9
1. *Time* (July 21, 1975).

Chapter 14
1. Tim Furniss, *Manned Spaceflight Log* (New York: Jane's Publishing, 1983).
2. *Aviation Week and Space Technology* (February 13, 1984).

GLOSSARY

aeronautics-the study of flight within the earth's atmosphere; including the areas of air-craft design and aerial navigation

astronautics-the study of flight outside the earth's atmosphere

astrophysics-the application of physical laws to celestial bodies and the space between them

attitude control-the system that regulates the position of a spacecraft in reference to its flight path

avionics-the application of electronics to the systems and equipment of aeronautics and astronautics

centrifugal force-the apparent force on a body forced to follow a curved path that tends to carry the body away from the center of rotation

drogue parachute-a small parachute that opens prior to, and helps to unfurl, the main parachute

hypersonic-five times the speed of sound or faster; roughly estimated at 3,500 MPH (5,600 km per hour)

jettison-to disconnect from a spacecraft and discard

micrometeoroid-particles of meteoric dust between 1 and 200 microns in diameter (1000 microns = 1 millimeter)

orbit-one body revolving around a primary body under the influence of the primary body's gravitational force alone

payload-any weight carried by a spacecraft above what is necessary for spaceflight; a spacecraft's working cargo

pressurization-containing air at a higher pressure than that around it; pressurized suits and pressurized cabins provide air in low-air or no-air conditions

propellant-the fuel for a rocket vehicle, which could also include oxidizers or additives to the fuel

retro-rockets-a small rocket whose thrust opposes a vehicle's forward motion in order to slow or stop the vehicle

simulators-a training machine that simulates actual flight situations, frequently with the aid of computers

supersonic-traveling faster than the speed of sound, which is roughly 760 MPH (1,216 km per hour) at sea level, less at higher altitudes

thrust-the propulsive force of a rocket or jet engine during firing

trajectory-the path of a body traveling because of external force

translation-the movement in a straight line without any rotation.

FOR FURTHER READING

Angelo, Jr., Joseph A. *The Dictionary of Space Technology*. NY: Facts On File, Inc., 1982.

Barbour, John. *Footprints on the Moon*. NY: Associated Press, 1969.

Benford, Timothy B., and Brian Wilkes. *The Space Program Quiz and Fact Book*. NY: Harper and Row, 1985.

Caidin, Martin. *The Man-in-Space Dictionary*. NY: E. P. Dutton, 1963.

Furniss, Tim. *Manned Spaceflight Log*. NY: Jane's Publishing, 1983.

Hallion, Richard P., and Tom D. Crouch, eds. *Apollo: Ten Years Since Tranquillity Base*. Washington: Smithsonian Institution Press, 1979.

Lewis, Richard S. *The Voyage of Apollo*. NY: Quadrangle/New York Times, 1974.

MacKnight, Nigel. *Shuttle*. Osceola, WI: Motorbooks International, 1985.

Moore, Patrick. *Space*. NY: Natural History Press, 1968.

Nayler, J. L. *A Dictionary of Astronautics*. Denver, CO: Hart Publishing, 1964.

O'Connor, Karen. *Sally Ride and the New Astronauts*. NY: Franklin Watts, Inc., 1983.

Osman, Tony. *Space History*. NY: St. Martin's Press, 1983.

Pioneering the Space Frontier: The Report of the National Commission on Space. NY: Bantam, 1986.

Powers, Robert M. *Shuttle: The World's First Spaceship*. Harrisburg, PA: Stackpole Books, 1979.

Rycroft, Michael, and David Shapland. *Spacelab: Research in Earth Orbit*. NY: Cambridge University Press, 1984.

Taylor, Jr., L. B. *Liftoff!* NY: E. P. Dutton, 1968.

Wilford, John Noble. *We Reach the Moon*. NY: New York Times, 1969.

Wolfe, Tom. *The Right Stuff*. NY: Farrar, Straus & Giroux, 1979.

INDEX

ABOUT
THE AUTHOR

Chris Crocker is a freelance journalist and author who writes about science, the arts, and the electronic media. A lifelong observer of the space program, Chris Crocker has been living and writing in Manhattan since 1977.